Praise for *Life's Too Short to Pretend You're Not Religious*

"Effectively skewering a central fallacy of the age, David Dark argues that at the deepest level no one is more or less religious than anyone else. With his premise granted, new avenues for ownership, responsibility, and attentiveness to all we say, do, and think arise. *Life's Too Short to Pretend You're Not Religious* is a call to consciousness and the compassion that accompanies the sacred insight that the whole world is kin and everything belongs."

—**Richard Rohr**, author of *Everything Belongs*

"For those of us who claim to be religious and those of us who religiously deny such labels, Dark grants the gift and burden to think deeply about the imagination, scaffolding, and consequences of our religiosity. In reading his journey and cautions, my sense of personal accountability and religious identity were expanded. Such is a book that reads the reader, and if we stick with it, we gain insight into self and neighbor."

—**Christina Edmondson**, scholar activist and host of *Truth's Table* podcast

"David Dark is one of our most astute and necessary cultural critics. His work gracefully opens new doors of understanding and breaks down barriers between secular and non-, and it puts a lot of old mythology out to pasture with a daring affirmation at the heart of his radical critique. *Life's Too Short* refreshingly ropes everyone in, insisting that we're all in it together. We often forget that."

—**Jessica Hopper**, author of *The First Collection of Criticism by a Living Female Rock Critic*

"David Dark's commitment to embracing the world whole makes him the sort of writer who can say in all seriousness but with a twinkle in his eye, 'I believe Radiohead.' It's a style that might not please readers who think fast food should never share a table with haute cuisine, but such readers are not the ones Dark seems to have in mind."

—**Maria Browning**, editor of *Chapter 16*

"Dark's book asks us to slow down and really consider how we label each other, how we look at ourselves, and how the religious impulse runs through all we do. If you're feeling a little worn down, and all the negative feelings that come with the word 'religious' rub you the wrong way, this book provides the fresh perspective you need."

—**Jen Rose Yokel**, The Rabbit Room

"Don't let an aversion toward that radioactive word dissuade you. *Life's Too Short to Pretend You're Not Religious* is a bracing manifesto for modern people and an optimism-infused love song to humanity. David Dark calls us to pay better, more generous attention to our own lives and the lives of others."

—**Sara Zarr**, National Book Award finalist and author of *The Lucy Variations*

"David Dark renders futile the cherished modern ambition to opt out of human religiosity; religion, rather, is a road we can make by walking with open eyes and informed minds. No marvels of progress can save us from being heretics and holy fools, or prophets, seers, and miracle workers. Dark helps us recognize these characters (and more) on the radio, in a dreary parking lot, and within ourselves."

—**Nathan Schneider**, journalist, professor of media studies at the University of Colorado Boulder, and author of *Everything for Everyone: The Radical Tradition That Is Shaping the Next Economy*

"David Dark reimagines being religious as a collective action open to all and demonstrates that in a time skeptical of religion, it can be a source of meaningful work and life-giving pleasure and joy—and even of change."

—**Kaya Oakes**, author of *The Defiant Middle* and
faculty member in the College Writing Programs at
University of California, Berkeley

"I am so very grateful for this book, which, among other things, demonstrates that answering 'Jedi' or 'Toni Morrison' when asked for your religious affiliation is a perfectly legitimate response to that question—thereby arguing us into another definition of what it means to be alive to wonder and mystery. And at a time in our culture when we seem to prefer our 'dialogues' to be conducted behind well-defended barricades from which we lob Twitter grenades, David Dark shows us that there could be another way to live with each other and speak with each other. Each sentence here is graced with a wisdom, humor, and humility that can't help but inspire us to be a little less suspicious of each other and to hope a little bit more—and if that isn't a rare gift of prophecy, I don't know what is."

—**Carlene Bauer**, author of *Frances and Bernard* and
Not That Kind of Girl

"Having read David Dark's book, I want to buy stock in Religion Unlimited, meaning that David helps us see why pronouncing religion dead or dying is shortsighted. The writing is muscular yet graceful, and the content is wise and insightful. You couldn't ask more from a book . . . and you couldn't ask for a more important subject."

—**Brian D. McLaren**, author, speaker, activist

"David Dark is one of the most important prophetic voices of our day. Not content to unravel the basic fabric of our existence, Dark reweaves the fibers into a rich and vibrant vision of the flourishing religious life for which we were created."

—**C. Christopher Smith**, founding editor of
The Englewood Review of Books

"Luminous reckonings with the real. The result is a shock of recognition. Here alone are the comedy and chaos that define the human condition and lead us gently, or not, into the strange new world of grace. An irresistible triumph."

—**Charles Marsh**, author of *Strange Glory:
A Life of Dietrich Bonhoeffer*

"This stuff is splendid, and it is David Dark more joyous and (dare I say it?) more upbeat than ever before. This is sheer gift. Pay attention."

—**Byron Borger**, reviewer and bookseller

Life's Too Short to Pretend You're Not Religious

REFRAMED + EXPANDED

David Dark

 Broadleaf Books

Minneapolis

For Rachel Masen

CONTENTS

INTRODUCTION

RELIGION HAPPENS

It wasn't their fault, it wasn't her fault.
It wasn't even a matter of fault.

—Elmore Leonard, *The Switch*

Religion names a thing. It matters how we name a thing.

Religion can ruin a perfectly good hang. For many of us, religion is the rock-solid reason we can't talk to our families. It stinks of brainwash. It shuts down imagination, intuition, and a healthy sense of oneself. Religion is a bullying mechanism that compels people to violate their own conscience. It's a mental contagion that gets hold of folks and won't let go, an industrial-strength conversation-stopper. A form, let's be honest, of weaponized despair. Religion names this horrible thing.

Religion can also be lovely sometimes. For many of us, religion is a call to somehow love and revere our families. It illuminates the threads of relationship. It's our access to forms of ancient intelligence summoning us to choose humility over hubris and love over fear. Religion is the moral memory of humankind. It is the lexicon of mystery, dressing the wounds of alienation, isolation, oppression, desertion, haste, and hierarchy. A form of love and longing. Religion names this beautiful thing.

To name a thing is to assert a kind of control over it. We need words with which to defend ourselves against the bad ideas that give rise to bad behavior. With a word like *religion*, I can get a fix on someone else's chaos, hit pause, freeze the frame, and hold it at what feels like a manageable angle. With a word like *religion*, I might also slow the tape on my own inner turmoil a little. Religion contains multitudes. We do too. Perhaps for a spell we might hold the thing we think we have in hand when we say *religion* at a different angle.

I come to you as one bummed out by the way many of us talk about religion. Be it an online rant, a headline, a news report, or a conversation overheard, religion, popularly deployed, compartmentalizes human behavior in a needlessly reductive way. I feel a jolt of sympathy pain whenever someone characterizes someone else as religious. It's as if a door just got slammed. A person has been somehow belittled, shrink-wrapped. Some sweet and perfectly interesting somebody got pushed to the side and left out. And in a subtle, hard-to-get-a-handle-on kind of way, they've been essentially shut up. Ever hear someone get referred to as too political, too polarizing, or beyond the pale? I have. And when *religious* gets affixed in a similarly demeaning fashion, it's a little triggering.

Consider: This is the way it goes with our words. When we label people, we no longer have to deal with them thoughtfully. We no longer have to feel overwhelmed by their complexity, the lives they live, the dreams they have. We know exactly where they are inside—or forever outside—our field of care because they've been *taken care of*. The mystery of their existence has been solved and filed away before we've had a chance to be moved by them or even begun to catch a glimpse of who they might be. We no longer need to listen to them because they've been neutralized. There's hardly any action quite so unde-manding, so utterly unimaginative, as the affixing of a label. It's the costliest of mental shortcuts.

Of course, we get to call it like we see it. What else can we do? But when we do so with undue haste, when we're neither remotely inquis-itive nor especially curious in our regard for other people, we may find that a casual demonization comes to pepper our conversations. This is why calling someone *progressive, conservative, fundamentalist, secular,* or *extremist* is to largely deal in curse words. It puts a person in what we take to be their place, but we're only speaking in shorthand. When I go no further in my consideration of my fellow human beings, I dis-play my preference for caricature over perception, a shrug as opposed to a vision of the lived fact of somebody in a body. In the face of a perhaps beautifully complicated life, I've opted for oversimplification. There's something too smooth in the way certain words can stop a train of thought.

And so it goes with the application of that impossibly broad brush called religion. It's as if we can't even speak the word without walking into the mine-field of someone else's wounds. Guards go up immediately and with good rea-son. It's a reservoir of toxicity, an asso-ciation to end all associations. Who would want to get caught anywhere near it? In certain contexts, *religious* tags someone as unsafe. A quick scan of most news cycles tells us why. Ostensibly religious people are often

And so it goes with the application of that impossibly broad brush called religion. It's as if we can't even speak the word without walking into the minefield of someone else's wounds.

the very folks who refuse to honor other people's boundaries in the thick of a global pandemic. And yet *religious*, if we aren't careful, can function as one more label we use as a placeholder of persons and populations, as if we've somehow gotten to the bottom of who they are with one adjective.

In this book, I want very much to take this attitude aside and punch it lovingly in the stomach. I want to slow the tape and see what's too easily hidden when we think we have people pegged. And if it's the case that mention of religion mostly shuts conversation down, I want to somehow crack it open again. I want to make the most of the word that, like *politics* and *media*, is among the most catastrophically unexamined abstractions of our time.

If we're open to it, *religion* need not always signal a dead end; it might even be a means to a breakthrough, a way of fessing up to the facts of what we're all up to, a way of highlighting—instead of obscuring—the sweet, loving, living fact of relationship, the deep-down interrelatedness we call life.

RELIGION AS PERCEIVED NECESSITY

In its root meaning, *religion* (from the Latin *religare*, "to bind again, to bind back") is simply a tying together, a question of how we see fit to organize ourselves and our resources, a question of how things have been tied together so far among two or more people *and* of how they might be tied together differently, a binding, an unbinding, and a binding again.

Because it's never static, religion is always up for grabs. It's dynamic that way. In fact, you can't step in the same religion twice because religion is a process. Or, more specifically, religion *names* a process.

Religion. Names. A. Process.

As has always been the case, the organizing of selves and societies can go beautifully or badly or something in between, but the development of bonds—like the dissolution of bonds—is inescapable. I find it most helpful to define religion, then, as follows:

Religion is perceived necessity; it is that which a person perceives as needful in their everyday thinking and doing.
Perceived necessity dictates speech, behavior, and, in a subtle way, that which we're prepared to let ourselves see. What I perceive as necessary decides my poses, my postures, and my positions. Perceived necessity directs where I sit and stand. And hear this: where we stand determines what we see.

There is no moral implied in this definition of religion. Perceived necessity is what it is, and there won't be a quiz. I deploy *religion* as a value-neutral term on purpose. By doing so, I can refer to the acted-upon desire for equal access to excellent public education for all young Americans as good religion. I can also refer to a refusal to wear a mask over a person's mouth and nose in an enclosed space when asked during a pandemic as bad religion.

See what I did there? I'm not conflating religion and politics exactly, but I *am* noting they're often two words for one thing: people figuring out what they think they owe each other and speaking and acting accordingly. Both words, *religion* and *politics*, come alive anew when we let them name cultures common to everyone. There's healthy religion and toxic religion and lots of religion of limited interest to most people. There are forms of perceived necessity that serve human thriving, and there are forms of perceived necessity that treat nature like a disposable ladder to heaven (in Robert Farrar Capon's phrase). Have you noticed?

A sense of perceived necessity is perhaps always in play. In these United States, for instance, some think it necessary to stand when the National Anthem is played or performed at a sporting event. Some are indifferent. Some think it more appropriate to kneel. A sense of what's appropriate, needful, and even sacred is afoot in our everyday doings, our sometimes largely unexamined ceremonies.

Unexamined, that is, until something shifts.

Colin Kaepernick famously sat during the National Anthem. After hearing and accepting word that a slightly different posture for signaling disapproval of the extrajudicial killing of Black people by law enforcement officials might prove less offensive to those enlisted or once enlisted within the US military, Colin Kaepernick even more famously decided to kneel. One small act of conscience undertaken by a famous person led to others.

Things escalated. Certain perceived necessities among the alleged leadership of the National Football League (NFL) were publicly laid bare. Other perceived necessities came into public view when the alleged leadership of Nike saw in Colin Kaepernick's story a solid platform with which they would be right to publicly partner in a series of ad campaigns. The one move from the one thoughtful man transformed into high geopolitical drama that's still showing us something about our perceived necessities. A political story? A sports story? It matters how we name a thing in our one human barnyard.

It happens that Colin Kaepernick has a Bible verse on his right arm. If, to your way of thinking, this detail somehow locks the story of his righteous witness down into a religion story, this book might not be for you. Religion doesn't suddenly make an entrance. Perceived necessities are always already there. Colin Kaepernick played along until he couldn't any longer. The story of his own sense of perceived necessity changed.

In the drive to compartmentalize (the drive to divide), there's no getting away from story. Stories change, but the fact of story doesn't. Story jumps the barricades of whatever it is we thought we had successfully cordoned off from something else. Stories often decline to follow the rules we've set up to protect one version of events from another. Our desperate need for stories sometimes beautifully and sometimes dangerously overcomes our need for propriety. "We tell ourselves stories in order to live," Joan Didion wrote. Ever find yourself caught up in one unexpectedly or against your better judgment?

When we escape a bad story—or see through one into the shock, the awe, or the absurdity of what's *really* going on—we haven't escaped stories; we've simply awakened our way into better and truer ones, and we've probably only managed that feat with the deeply attentive, con siderate assistance of others, whether living or dead. No one awakens all by themselves. Conversions occur all the time. For better *and* worse, we change our minds. We find ourselves wanting to identify with a kneeling athlete. The question of justice comes into view. Certain postures we were once prone to assume are no longer acceptable to us. Before we know it, we're trying to get in on the act lest we miss the righteous movements happening around us and we can no longer live with ourselves. We get pulled in. People drink the proverbial Kool-Aid. Religion happens.

We're often admonished to keep religion out of politics (or vice versa), and civil exchange does require that no one be allowed to hog the microphone while decreeing or successfully insinuating that the God in their head trumps the reasoning power in everyone else's. After all, abusive behavior marketed or pushed in court as religious freedom is still abusive behavior. There are limits to the right to religion. Including when people don't respect boundaries. Keep your religion to yourself. Your politics too.

But human life won't divide itself up quite so neatly. Given the overwhelming complications of trying to negotiate a just, joyful, and more-helpful-than-not existence in a world of raw data with which we often have no idea what to do, we can perhaps be forgiven for wanting to rope off one issue from the other. ("That's political. That's religious. That's a private matter. This is worship. That's a guilty pleasure. And this one over here is just . . . it's just business. It is what it is. It's nothing personal. Sorry about that.") But these divisions can obscure the living fact of certain connections and leave us estranged from our own sense of ourselves, insulated from the possibility of undivided living. There's a time for compartments, but my desire to compartmentalize my own words and actions doesn't serve the deeper hope—the better, more beautiful story—of a unified life, one marked by a sense of wholeness, sustainability, and constancy.

If we're willing, at least on occasion, to apply the word *religion* to the whole of our own lives as readily as we level it at others, it can

If we're willing, at least on occasion, to apply the word *religion* to the whole of our own lives as readily as we level it at others, it can wonderfully disrupt whatever it was we thought we were talking about.

wonderfully disrupt whatever it was we thought we were talking about, whatever we thought we had in mind and hand. Like *culture*, it cuts to the core of what we're really doing and believing, of what values—we all have them—lurk behind our words and actions. Yes, we can use the word to disavow and detract. ("I *used* to be religious." "I'm spiritual but not religious." "Let's keep religion out of it.") But there's something evasive and detached at work if we mean to suggest it's only other people who are sometimes guided by unreasoning rage or strange notions about the way the world works, only others who have an agenda. In this view, *religion* is only a word for the way other people get carried away—a snob's word. Sometimes it's a strange disowning of one's own vulnerability and, if you like, gullibility. In some instances, it can function as a rude denial of the fact of our common creatureliness.

My fellow creatures, I propose we not play that way. If what we believe is what we see is what we do is who we are, there's no getting away from the question posed by the word *religion*. We all want to know who we are, where and how we fit in, and what our lives might yet mean. And in this sense, *religion* might often be the best word we have for seeing, naming, confessing, and really waking up to what we're after in all we do, of becoming aware of what's going on in our minds. Putting religion openly on the table in this way might transform it into the most pressing, interesting, and wide-ranging conversation we can have. We might even find ourselves amused.

How's that? Because religion can radically name the specific ways we've put our lives together and, perhaps more urgently, the ways we've allowed other people to put our lives together for us. And no, I'm not trying to champion an abstraction or an adjective here. I'm not trying to talk anyone into self-identifying *as* religious (as futile and redundant a move as calling yourself *political* or *cultural*). But I *am* arguing that we should cease and desist from referring to others as *religious* as if they're participants in games we ourselves aren't in any way invested in, as if they're somehow weirdly and hopelessly enmeshed in cultures of which we're always only detached observers. Not only is it a distancing move that risks holding ourselves aloof, detached from the fact of our own enthusiasms, our own rituals, our own enmeshments, and our own loves, but it also holds another person—the ostensibly religious person—under a scrutiny we perhaps have yet to apply to ourselves. Calling someone else *religious*, if we aren't careful, can serve as a form of deflection, of avoiding the question of our own investments, our own perceived necessities.

RELIGION AS RELATIONSHIP

To be genuinely attentive to the question of religion is to see relationally, to examine the stories we inherit and hand down to others without too much thought as well as those we cobble together to work a crowd, fund a campaign, target a market, justify a drone strike, or convince ourselves to get out of bed in the morning. Some sociologists invite us to form the words *belief systems* around these phenomena. Doing so can prove profoundly helpful in the work of achieving a degree of critical distance when it comes to our perceived have-tos. ("Our belief systems may differ here and there, but we both want better public schools, right? *Right.*") And in the age-old task of listening sympathetically to our fellow creatures, of imagining them well, we need all the help we can get. Thank you, social science.

But I'm not sure anyone's ever experienced enlightenment, been born again, been called to repentance, or decided to sell their belongings on account of a system. The voice, the tale, the image, the parable that gets through to you—that *wins your heart*—is the one that makes it past your defenses. You've been won over, and you probably didn't see it coming. You've been enlisted into a drama, whether positively or negatively, and it shouldn't be controversial to note that it happens all the time. When you really think about it, there's one waiting around every corner. It's as near as the story, song, or image you can't get out of your head.

Religion happens when we get pulled in, moved, called out, or compelled by something outside ourselves. It could be a car commercial, a lyric, a painting, a theatrical performance, or the magnetic pull of an Apple store. The calls to worship are everywhere. And when we see as much, we begin to understand why Karl Marx insisted that "the critique of religion is the prerequisite of every critique."[1] It is the way we do everything we do or think we do. It is certainly often an opiate for the masses, but it can also function as the poetry of the people. Whether we spy it in ritual, symbol, or ceremony, religion isn't something one can be coherently for or against or decide to somehow suddenly engage, because it's always already there. Or as the old Palmolive commercial once put it, we're *soaking* in it. Whatever the content of the scripts we're sticking to for dear life—that would be our religion—it binds us for worse or for better till we begin to critique it religiously and relentlessly, in view of the possibility of conversion to better boundedness, different and more redeeming orientations, or, to put it a little strangely, *less bad* religion.

A person's religiosity is never not in play. It names the patterns, shifting or consistent, avowed or not, of all our interactions. Religion is the question of how we dispose our energies, how we see fit to organize our own lives and, in many cases, the lives of others.

This need be neither buzzkill nor bummer. Genuinely critical thinking about religion is a lovely opportunity, an invitation to be more present in our own lives, to access and examine more deeply what it is that we're up to. Good analysis shows relationship. Bad analysis obscures it. Go granular or go home.

Defining religion as perceived necessity serves the ends of thoughtfulness. It also levels the playing field more than a little because suddenly a Muslim going to prayers isn't more or less religious than a grown man with a big piece of pretend cheese on his head going to watch a Green Bay Packers game. Is it good religion? Bad religion? True? False? Idolatrous? Righteous? Opinions will vary. But to hit pause long enough to consider *the content* of our devotion, our lives, and our investments is to begin to see the questions clearly. What are my perceived necessities? Do I like the stories my one life tells? Do I need to see about changing them?

Defining religion as perceived necessity serves the ends of thoughtfulness. It also levels the playing field.

There are no firewalls in these matters. We're never *not* speaking or acting upon our religion. We're always in the thick of it, this living fact of what our human hands have wrought under the dictation of what's actually going on in our human hearts and minds. Our real sense of what's really sacred is regularly on display. Musician-writer David Byrne bears witness to this everyday apocalypse when he invites us to consider the cities. Having made a regular habit of biking through as many as he can as often as he can while on tour, he describes his ongoing realization that cities are nothing less than the "physical manifestations of our deepest beliefs and our often unconscious thoughts." It's merely a matter of recognition: "A cognitive scientist need only look at what we have made—the hives we have created—to know what we think and what we believe to be important. . . . It's all there, in plain view, right out in the open."

We evade. We compartmentalize. We say *this* doesn't have anything to do with *that*. But what we're up to isn't, as it turns out, a secret: "You don't need CAT scans and cultural anthropologists to show you what's going on inside the human mind; its inner workings are manifested in three dimensions." Our religion is alarmingly self-evident if we're open to taking a hard look around. Consider the hives: "Our values and hopes are sometimes awfully embarrassingly easy to read. They're right there—in the storefronts, museums, temples, shops, and office buildings. . . . They say, in their unique visual language, 'This is what we think matters, this is how we live and how we play.'"[2]

NO COMMUNION WITHOUT NUANCE

Like God, the economy, or the devil, religion is in the details. Like any artist, Byrne would have us begin to think harder about what we're going through, to lean into the fact of certain connections we're in the weird habit of denying, to move through the world with our antennae out, saying—or singing—what we see. To do so artfully is to engage in the kind of poetic thinking we associate with Byrne or any creative personality determined to be awake and alive to the myths in which we otherwise swim unknowingly, myths in which we've been immersed so long that they've become second nature to us, myths by and through which we've measured our lives so unconsciously that we've forgotten how arbitrary they are, myths from which we're perfectly free to withdraw our consent when we begin to ask ourselves, "Well, how did we get here?"

To genuinely ask this kind of question is to take up the task of philosophy, the love of wisdom, which is said to begin with wonder. To be a philosopher is to be a practitioner of artful self-awareness, a way of wondering at ourselves and all the strange things we put up with, sustain, and perpetuate, a way of bringing it all to consciousness. What task could be more urgent for a person?

When we let religion name our lived commitments, avowed *and* unavowed, acknowledged *and* obscured, it can begin to serve as one of the farthest-reaching, readily available concepts for looking hard and honestly at our own lives, for *really* leveling with ourselves, and for abandoning our dysfunctional ideas for better ones, truer, livelier, more sustainable ways of negotiating our existence. It is in this sense that it might be helpful to voice a few interlocking provocations:

> Life's too short to pretend we're not in relationship.
>
> Life's too short to pretend we're not political.
>
> Life's too short to pretend we're not religious.

I speak this way in the hope of holding space for a deeper discernment of certain connections too often obscured when we speak as if our preferred compartments are airtight realities. I'm also trying to challenge the binary thinking that insists—and sometimes even forcibly decrees—that one thing has nothing to do with the other. I want to hold the tension between alleged opposites to see what we might behold there. If we can slow our roll a little when it comes to the words, ideas, and people we imagine—sometimes needlessly—to be in opposition to one another, certain insights come into view. If I can, I'd like to propose *re*membering wherever someone has successfully posited a *dis*membering dualism or dichotomy.

Why do I want to frame the conversation this way? I'm in it for beauty. As someone who has dared to try to teach people for most of my adult life, I often suspect that what I'm up to is, in large part, an effort to try to stop people from becoming bored and giving up too soon, to help them find their own lives and the lives of others powerfully interesting, weird, and somehow beautiful. I believe pop music, for instance, often functions as wisdom literature. I believe, with Keats, in the holiness of the heart's affections. I think there's poetic intelligence pulsing within so much that we love and are drawn to without always knowing how to say why. I think there's information in our anger, our binge-watching, and our mood swings.

Look again, *re*spect, stay with the information, and consider the possibility that there might be more going on in a neighbor, a novel, an image, or a conversation overheard than your mind had grasped the first time around, something worthy of your time, something beautiful.

The "willingness continually to revise one's own location in order to place oneself in the path of beauty is the basic impulse underlying education,"[3] wrote Elaine Scarry. This defines education as a journey but also as a creative task that involves finding and seeing beauty in the very places where we've grown accustomed to only sensing and feeling conflict. True education requires responding to conflict with curiosity, as Pádraig Ó Tuama instructs.[4] Where *religion* has rightly served as a word to name and thereby control concentrated, communal toxicity, this kind of beautiful education models a way of approaching with a little less oppositional energy[5] and considerably less fear. If I can, I'd like to somehow conjure this kind of relaxed and less-fearful space for seeing more clearly what we're up to and longing for.

Which brings us back to religion as a divider. In my work as an educator, I seek to challenge the ease with which we succumb to the false divide of labels, that moment in which our empathy gives out and we refuse to respond openhandedly or even curiously to people with whom we differ. As I see it, to refuse the possibility of finding another person interesting, complex, and as complicated as oneself is a form of violence. At bottom, this is a refusal of nuance, which I posit as sacred. To call nuance sacred is to value it so much and esteem it so highly that we find it fitting to somehow set it apart as something to which we're forever committed. Nuance refuses to envision others degradingly, refuses denying them the content of their own experience, even as it talks us down tenderly from the false ledges we've put ourselves on. When we take it on as a sacred obligation, nuance also delivers us out of the deadly habit of cutting people out of our own imaginations. This opens us up to the possibility of at least occasionally finding one another beautiful, the possibility of communion. I live for these openings, and I suspect I write "NUANCE" as request and reminder in the margins of research papers more than any other word. It could be that there's no communion without it.

By *communion*, I mean not a retreat from the everyday or the realistic but a more profound engagement with it. This profound engagement holds true to Iris Murdoch's definition of *love*: "Love is the extremely difficult realisation that something other than oneself is real. Love, and so art and morals, is the discovery of reality."[6]

The work of critical consciousness, we begin to understand, is never done. It's a moral task worthy of a lifetime. Like art and song and dance, it's a party to which everyone, living or dead or yet to come, is invited. A river of life to all who seek it.

RELIGION IS WITNESS

I hope to hold space for conceiving religion along a moral spectrum. Thinking critically, for instance, is good religion. Suppressing speech is bad religion. Good religion, wherever it arises, is a way of getting unstuck from our failures of imagination in the way we see ourselves and others, getting unstuck from bad religion, wherever it arises; those mean mental habits by which we casually, definitively deny kinship with neighbors, strangers, family, incarcerated persons, enemy combatants, asylum seekers, or most anyone who might disturb our defensive sense of our own identities. Letting religion name all our own perceived necessities and the ways we pursue them allows us to open our lives to an ever-renewed perception and recognition of our profoundly interdependent relationship to the rest of the world. I view true religion as a summons to see ourselves anew *and* to discover reality as it is—not *making* connections exactly, because the truth is they're already there, preceding us as the very facts on the ground, whether we recognize them or not. To begin to respond to such a summons is to enter the kind of accountability—the deep awareness—that occurs when we see and think poetically, because poetry is the work of recognition, the work of seeing beautifully.

We lose no ground when we note that there are myriad ways to be true. We might even gain something in the way of candor, ownership, transparency, and substance if we can fess up to our own devotions.

What manner of devotee art thou?

What's the what, the how, and the why of your day-to-day?

Let's hold our devotions out with open hands. Or as Leonard Cohen so memorably put it, let us compare mythologies.

It's a life's work for sure, but with humor and compassion, we can try to own what we're up to; we can try to be true in all we do.

Your obsession with the Marvel cinematic universe? Religious.

Your determination to hold on to that plastic bottle till you've found a recycling receptacle? Religious.

The song you sing when you're alone? Religious.

Your response to your fellow pilgrim who just cut you off in traffic? Religious.

The bad ideas you're leaving behind *and* the new ones you're trying on? Religious.

We're always showing our perceived necessities. They're plain as day. Or to borrow a phrase from Jesus of Nazareth, we'll be known by our "fruit"—what those perceived necessities enact. The operative term—the excruciatingly helpful word I have in mind here—is *witness*. There is no on-and-off switch when it comes to my witness. When it comes to yours. It's simply the evidence of my output. My witness is the sum of everything I do and leave undone. The words are there, but the actions speak louder.

Our witness isn't what we say we believe or even what we think we believe. It isn't the image, pose, or posture we try to present to others. It's what we do, what we give, what we take, and what we actually bring to our little worlds. In some sense, the future will know what our witness was better than we can, the ways we rang true (or didn't). Time's the revelator when it comes to what your religion is, what your witness is or, as it turns out, was. Your religion is your witness is the shape your love and your hate takes. In all things.

And before I go too far asking you or anyone else to consider the ups and downs of their weird religious background, I'd like to devote some space to describing, as best as I can, my own. For every hero or villain, there's always an origin story. There's always religion. Here's hoping that our neuroses might also be, in some deep sense and from time to time, our communal wisdom. I'll go first.

1

CRACKERS AND GRAPE JUICE

People who can't make the world into a story, go mad.
—Ursula K. Le Guin

Picture an '80s-era seventeen-year-old in horn-rimmed glasses and a maroon vest sitting in a box office, waiting for a late-night movie audience to appear. It could have been *The Princess Bride* or *Top Gun* or *No Way Out*. The responsibility that befell me was to sell tickets, eat popcorn, and talk to customers about the only thing I really wanted to talk about anyway. I asked strangers what their favorite movies were to help them come to a decision, and they'd thank me for sharing my expertise. Conversations never ended quite so beautifully among my peers, but here, I'd found my people.

But on this particular evening, I'd forgotten something. I knew it was a Sunday and felt a little bit bad about having *labored* on it. I had an image of my grandfather, a lifelong Tennessee farmer located near the Mississippi border, reading his newspaper in a rocking chair, attired in his Sunday best till the sun went down and it seemed to him permissible to feed the mules. But it wasn't too long since we'd visited and watched television together, so I felt sufficiently on task and in sync with my people. This was something else.

At about a quarter to midnight, I suddenly realized I was staring down the barrel of having missed, for the first Sunday since my baptism, "taking Communion," or what my tradition called the Lord's Supper, and this was decidedly *not* okay. Nobody had spelled out such quandaries to me explicitly, but in my head, such negligence could potentially constitute a kind of cosmic deal breaker. Partaking of the Lord's Supper was my way of re-upping on the forgiveness of sins on a weekly basis. If I skipped it even once, there was the lurking feeling that my scarlet-stained soul would *not* be rendered white as snow. Try as I might, I couldn't get it out of my mind. Feigning calm, I asked a coworker to mind the shop and made for the door.

If you had been in Nashville at a nearby Kroger in 1987, you might have witnessed an anxious, wing-tipped young man running up and down the aisles searching desperately for Saltine crackers and Welch's grape juice. Once past the register, I made my way briskly toward the exit and paused in the parking lot to say a quick prayer to the God who, as far as I could tell, appeared to demand these things. I stared at the starry sky above as I wolfed down the crackers and juice with seconds remaining till midnight and laughed to myself. I'd made it . . . for now.

If you find this ridiculous. Pitiful. Horribly sad. I'd like to say that I do, too, even as I still feel deep kinship with this confused young person. His ability to find *himself* ridiculous and to laugh at his own thinking saves the scene, in my view, and renders the situation a little less tragic. When I wonder how it is that a crazed fundamentalist like me could laugh at

I stared at the starry sky above as I wolfed down the crackers and juice with seconds remaining till midnight.

himself at a moment like that, I find myself back at the movie theater, that bastion of story and song where so many an epiphany has come to me my whole life long. Truth be told, I wasn't, strictly speaking, alone in that parking lot. In my mind, there were others.

I couldn't help but wonder, for instance, what Steve Martin, for whom I felt and continue to feel a kind of very remote love, might make of my passionate performance. And as earnest and afraid as I was, I certainly couldn't deny that my trembling ingestion of juice and crackers would fit perfectly in an episode of my beloved *Twilight Zone*. And were the crew of the starship *Enterprise* to stumble upon an individual on some lonely planet where getting the timing right on such a ritual was ascribed such earth-shattering significance, it seemed to me that Captain Kirk might think it needful, one more time, to refuse the counsel of Mr. Spock and go ahead and violate the prime directive for poor, poor pitiful me, for mercy's sake. There was also Doctor Who to think about. I could well imagine a centuries-old Time Lord from Gallifrey helping me regard my lonely, beleaguered self with more candor, clarity, and compassion than came to me easily in that moment.

My bemused laughter, you begin to understand, arose from a certain not-at-all-aloneness I owed to a great cloud of pop-culture witnesses surrounding me, affording me more than a few fragments to shore up against my psychological ruin.

SPOT THE SENSITIVE ONE

A month or two later, I made my way to a friend's eighteenth birthday party. His parents were divorced, and the celebration was at his father's place. It was a guys-only affair.

We all stood around the kitchen talking about being seniors and applying to colleges while going to work on Doritos and soft drinks.

There was a giggle every so often about a special surprise in store for us that evening, and the few who appeared to be in the know would exchange wide-eyed looks before changing the subject to add to the suspense. My friend's father would smile and shake his head. In time, there came a knock at the door. It was opened to reveal a woman in a trench coat who was, if memory serves, smiling.

Thanks to a senior English project, I'd been reading Dostoevsky novels all year and was lately in the habit of concluding that I alone, like some sensitive Russian monk, could be expected to hold to the standard of genuine humanness in scenes of tragic degradation. Add to this a certain sanctimoniousness, and you can imagine how bewildered and blindsided I felt at the nearness of an affable woman completely bare but for strategically placed tassels required by Tennessee state law. I felt mortified. As perfunctory cheers, whistles, and the forced-sounding laughter of my peers mercifully compensated for my sudden silence, I politely declined the offer to place a five-dollar bill between hip and elastic and negotiated a swift exit.

Feeling more than a little estranged from my friends and that I might have failed them in some way by not sticking around, I turned on the tape deck in my mother's Caprice Classic and was greeted by the weird and welcome world of a treasured Tom Waits cassette. Barreling down the interstate listening to "Hang On St. Christopher" off *Franks Wild Years* did not render the universe or my role within it any less problematic, but it did have me feeling less left out of things and even a tiny bit vindicated. According to my antagonized imagination, a raspy-voiced, world-weary, imaginative man like Waits represented certain otherwise unavailable sympathies. It was as if he'd forgotten more than my rowdy friends would ever know, and he was on *my* side—worried over the kinds of things that worried me and alive to certain contradictions and hypocrisies I was also determined to be alive to. Tom Waits got me, I felt, as if we were somehow a tragicomedy team of two, navigating strange feelings and difficult situations artfully.

Perhaps this is the way it works for many of us. We try on postures and personas, voices and songs. We look for witnesses with whom to measure and inform, reconsider, and revise our own lives. I wasn't simply amused or entertained by Tom Waits (or Captain Kirk or Doctor Who). I was, and I am, in no small way devoted to him. He had me at the growly "Hello" of a music video in which he came at me as a bleary, strangely contented bedraggled-looking man in a prop room singing to a mannequin through a bullhorn.

Listening to him, I felt beckoned to see my own life and the lives of others differently, called out to see what he's showing, the strange, sideways view of reality he posits, a view in which everything is weirdly connected to everything else. I still find Waits—he's in the *showing* business, after all—completely and utterly convincing. His witness enriches my own. In truth, the mere thought of him helps me overcome my own timidity.

Years later, on a long car drive, I played Tom Waits for my five-year-old son. His admiring assessment of Waits's voice formed within seconds: "He sounds like he's already dead." The circle will, I think, be unbroken.

THIS HAS TO DO WITH THAT

This brings me back to Steve Martin and Rod Serling's *The Twilight Zone* and how they arose in the mind of the nervy young fellow trying to avert God's wrath in a Kroger parking lot. We have, on the one hand, a teenage lifetime of sermons and Sunday school curriculums, and all the weird fears I figured were backed up in the Bible somewhere. And on the other, there was a hodgepodge of reading, listening, television viewing, stories, *Saturday Night Live* and *SCTV* skits, stand-up routines, songs, and videos through which my friends and

I tried to make sense of ourselves and find patterns to live by. I dwelt, like I imagine everyone does, in the tension between what I was into and what I was supposed to be into.

But mercifully, in my view, this tension was never definitively resolved. I learned to love, lean into, and even make a living of examining it. I never bought into the notion that Sunday mornings and the rest of the week belonged in different hands or that I was somehow dealing with everlastingly competing truths. I couldn't quite draw that kind of line, given the fact, for instance, that I remember the day of my baptism mostly because *Superman II* aired on ABC that night. I had yet to hear of a secular and sacred divide, but then as now, it dissolved upon contact with the way my heart works.

I had—and have—before me a wide array of references to regulate my inner dramas, whether a poem, a scene in a David Lynch film, a Kendrick Lamar lyric, a Bible verse, or a scene from *Squid Game*. I have many strands with which to build and rebuild my web of meaning—I do it without thinking about it—and many means to reconnect when disconnection occurs. Many advocates, real and imagined, beckon me back when I suspect I've decisively strayed from what's righteous and real.

Consider again the grape juice and crackers in my trembling hands and my desperate hold on what I thought might prove to be a cosmically costly loose end. I didn't want to live in a world where, in a moment like that, my enthusiasms weren't allowed to address me, as if my crisis was so narrowly religious that it somehow sealed me off from the rest of the human world and all its saving associations.

I badly needed to overcome this artificial divide. I still do. I want a wide-open world made new, again and again, by bigger and better pictures of who I am and what I might yet be.

I badly needed to overcome this artificial divide. I still do.

I want a wide-open world made new, again and again, by bigger and better pictures of who I am and what I might yet be. Perhaps this is a desire common to everyone.

To begin to take stock of my own multitude of counselors, to affirm that a film or a comic book has been a means of grace, to name the voices I depend upon to make better and more artful sense of myself and others—why not see what all's in there? Why not hold it out with open hands?

COMMON HUMAN CULTURE

Recall again that religion *is* rebinding, that tying together of the ties that bind us, whether for good or ill. And the question of religion is the question of who and what we're bound to, how it is we find ourselves tied up, and what our biggest big ideas actually are, the ideas to which we find ourselves helplessly, unknowingly, or even gratefully attached. Whether we have in mind a highlight or a hang-up, a recurrent anxiety or an ecstatic epiphany, religion names our social bonds.

> **The question of religion is the question of who and what we're bound to, how it is we find ourselves tied up, and what our biggest big ideas actually are.**

Understandably, there are very solid reasons for resisting such a broad conception of what religion means. Many among us feel so damaged by the spiritual abuse of our upbringing, so embarrassed by the strange and outrageous things we only recently believed so fervently, that the word serves wonderfully well for drawing a line between brainwash and rational thought.

I'm not religious signals firmly that I'm done. I'm not falling for that backward madness anymore, and I won't be made to sit quietly when someone starts singing that sad, confusing song. It also conjures a little distance between cool reason and the crazies.

Spiritual? Sure. But religious—those awkward people who only speak in monologue in the unfortunate habit of mistaking the voice of God for the voice in their heads and then acting accordingly? We know too well how it goes when those who are religious hold elected office, sit on school boards, or storm the Capitol in the strong name of Jesus. They destroy our hopes for an otherwise sensibly secular scene in which people are people, appeals to reason aren't punished, and nobody plays the God card. Why ruin everything with religion? Isn't coming out of it alive what evolution is for?

Believe me, I get it. There's no abuse like "faith-based" abuse. In America, membership in church organizations seems to serve as political capital for white supremacist terror operatives in every area of public life. Some of the most publicly abusive figures in our news cycles claim a generalized "faith" and tweet Bible verses while morally debasing themselves to accrue cred and coin. And needless to say, many churches are only as honest as their wealthiest members. The God grift is real.

But why let grifters define terms? It seems to me that too much is at stake to sit the argument out. We surrender too much rhetorical ground to bad actors when religion *only* names toxic forms of faith and practice. To claim to be "anti-religious," without getting into the specifics of any tradition, is to shake a fist at an impossibly large target. Religion, in this sense, is a concept too general to be meaningfully *for* and too abstract to be coherently *against*. Taking a stand *against* religion in general is no more sensible than being opposed to promises, the forming of a line at Starbucks, or the power of association. Being *for* it is as strange a conviction as delighting in mobs, mass hysteria, or assemblies. To believe we can successfully undertake either is to be stunningly inattentive to the wonderfully complicated offerings of our common human culture.

There is no religion in general. Why waste energy opposing an abstraction when we're free to slow the tape and speak with specificity and care?

There's a less radioactive way of talking about these things—back to witness: the actual content of someone's allegedly religious activity (volunteering in a soup kitchen, executing an adulterer, fasting for immigration reform, burning a flag, or physically attacking someone who's decided to do so). Religion is no more necessarily harmful or harmless than, say, an angle of vision. "Religions are places to stand and look and act," author Neil Gaiman wrote, "vantage points from which to view the world."[1] But even if we're all situated—seeing, speaking, and acting from and within a particular vantage point—there has to be a certain fluidity at play. When it comes to traditions, for instance—and there is no religion without them—they're always changing, dying, and coming back to life.

Tradition (from the Latin *tradere*, "to transfer") is simply that which has passed down the pipeline, the stories and images we only truly inherit through redeployment. Old ceremonies are practiced anew in unforeseen contexts, taking on fresh new meaning. The life of traditions *is* their mobility. They're handed down, passed around, borrowed from, and mulled upon. They're as varied and divided as their supposed adherents. In this sense, traditions are religions so dynamic and in process that we can't nail one down or, as much as we'd like to think we could, somehow analyze one definitively. A tradition is a process. To urge a possibly helpful axiom again, you can't step in the same religion twice.

As a young fellow trying to perform a sacred ritual in a parking lot, I was in desperate need of a little mobility, a more fluid take on my own religious situation than I'd had up until then (which read thus: be baptized and consume crackers and juice with due reverence on the first day of each week, and you'll probably escape eternal torment). Somehow, and I know it doesn't go this way for everyone—my laughter and Tom Waits showed me—I knew I didn't need to be all hemmed in alone, stuck, afraid, and isolated with my debilitating ideas about God and eternity. My vantage point remained blessedly porous enough to admit the influence of other voices, other vantage points that came to my aid to help me find myself funny, weird, and not entirely alone. Despite my real fear of eternal conscious pain, I remained open to imagined interlocutors. They gave me permission to feel and think differently. They helped me stop shrinking the world down to the size of my own fears.

HUNTING AND GATHERING

Having felt free—and even called—to dabble widely, it would be difficult to think of my religious background as a crime that was carried out against me. Many understandably do. I imagine I would, too, if I viewed it narrowly, only meaning what I took it to mean in my especially confused moments as a teenager. In my struggle to make sense of myself and to distinguish between what's real and what's not, my take on the tradition doesn't center, as it once did, around anxiety concerning the afterlife. These days, Christianity is one sacred, communal movement among many. More, it often manifests as the freshening flow of an effort fluid and alive enough to mean more than what I had reduced it to. As I see it, Christianity is transparency, or it's nothing at all. It's a living process, a complicated legacy that, when improperly handled, can do great harm.

It would be a while before I knew how to put it this way. But in the meantime, the art of music, literature, and film were there to let a little air in. They spiritually formed me—and even saying that doesn't do justice to the gift of awareness they give me. To speak of art as a side issue is to distort the fact of the situation. Why keep the poetic and the prophetic unartfully separated from one another? The stories and songs that entrance and give us life, that nurture and nourish our souls, that render us more attentive to the lives we're living—what are they if not religious?

"People who can't make the world into a story, go mad," novelist Ursula K. Le Guin observed. Always I'm on a pilgrimage of hunting and gathering whatever I can find that might help me cobble together a more inspiringly coherent account of my own experience, reaching for anything, really, that might somehow illumine my darkness. As a young boy, this took the form of a devotion to the Incredible Hulk, King Kong, and probably any strong, misunderstood creature whose displacement led to the destruction of property. I am one who, as a child, once labored on a vivid, colorful, and detailed picture of Godzilla with his name emblazoned in large capital letters, presented it humbly to his grandmother, and had it handed back immediately with the decree, "There's only one God." Message received. *That* can't have anything to do with *this*. The stark divide.

I imagine these mean little dichotomies being dropped on children young and old the world over, and I hope to bring an end to them whenever I can. I get worked up when I sense this form of bullying is going on, when I read it on faces or hear it echoing in the voices of folks who seem reluctant or ill-equipped to discuss these matters. I come by my determined, lifelong refusal of these divisions honestly. It's a matter of personal sanity. If undivided vision goes, then meaning, coherence, and a loving future go with it. I want everything connected to everything else, a sacred whole. I want everyone to know their own moral power.

Of course, the casual squashing of a child's living imagination isn't the sum total of the peculiar inheritance vouchsafed unto me. There were also many matters of conscience that got instilled—mostly blessedly—early on. The grandmother of whom I speak would correct me if, upon parting, I presumed aloud I'd see her again come Christmas. "*If the Lord wills*, we will see each other again," she would intone in macabre fashion with raised eyebrows. Perhaps incontestably the handing down of a hang-up, but, for my part, I wouldn't be quick to trade it away, even as I'm careful to avoid passing these obsessions over wholesale to my children.

WISDOM AND NEUROSIS

A religious background, whatever form it takes, is a mixed bag. My grandmother's often domineering determination never to speak or allow an idle word had at least a root or two in those ancient communal efforts toward wholeness and healing we call sacred traditions. Let your "yes" mean yes and your "no" mean no, and anything extra—a vow, for instance—is manipulative filler or toxic denial of your own finitude, a claim to know more than you can personally guarantee. Maybe this is a tradition worthy of maintaining: say what you mean. Simply name the ongoing process whereby we parse out what we've inherited: the true, the real, and the life-giving, or the dysfunctional, degrading, and death-dealing. Traditions are everywhere. Throw a rock and you'll hit one.

When it comes to this particular Dark family tradition of watching one's language, I have a similar relationship with the idle word. Say I'm late to class, and in an attempt at humor, I apologize and say I had to snap the neck of an assassin, or that parking was complicated by the fact that I rode into work on a Ferris wheel, or that Daniel Day-Lewis won't stop texting me. Even when I know my students know I'm just goofing around, I feel obliged to whisper almost inaudibly, "Just kidding." It's as if I can't release an untruth into the air without feeling the need to swat it down somehow.

Is this habit only a centimeter away from the young lunatic in the parking lot? Well, okay, but it's my inheritance, and I'm trying to make the most of it. It can be a salubrious quirk as well as a source of paranoia and entertainment. As much as it complicates things, a legacy of trying very hard not to lie isn't a bad way to live. Either way, there it sits. As ever, our neuroses and our wisdom are closely aligned.

PLEASE OPEN YOUR BIBLES

This is also the case in my lifelong relationship of love and fear, assurance and anxiety, when it comes to the Bible. I used to worry about placing other books on top of it lest it appear to have been marginalized. I'd read it all the way through—or at least made sure my eyes passed over each word—at a very early age for fear of what might become of me if I got caught dead without having done so. Better safe than sorry, my logic went. The same reasoning was applied in the mental gymnastics I carried out in an effort to assure myself and others that the entire thing was void of contradiction.

At the age of sixteen, I preached a sermon that hinged on the scene in Luke's Gospel where a dying man crucified beside Jesus asks to be remembered by him when he enters his kingdom. Jesus tells him, "Today you will be with me in Paradise." A moving exchange in itself, my need to know quickly shifted past the exchange to ensuring the Bible was consistent and that everything within it added up appropriately into one unified doctrine. Now this extension of a saving word to a man about whom we knew almost nothing constituted a problem. What to do?

Well, make it work. It's all very simple, I explained. Because the Bible is without contradiction, we can infer that this thief was probably among the multitude baptized by John the Baptist and can safely assume that Jesus, either through omniscience or a kind of built-in baptism scanner, was capable of knowing as much as he gazed upon him. Otherwise, he would have known not to say such a thing. Problem solved.

It's embarrassing—but instructive—to note that this is the troubled spot where I've lived a sizable chunk of my life. I don't claim to have evolved beyond all embarrassing ideological commitments. If I'm blessed with a long enough life, I hope and pray that I'll look back with fondness on my fifty-two-year-old, well-meaning, but woefully narrow-minded, Bible-reading self. As much as the sixteen-year-old self. Though I'd like to think I don't cling to my own interpretations quite so nervously and defensively as I once did, but who's to say?

There was a time when I was suspicious of commentary and footnotes, as if they were a grossly human hindrance to God's direct communication with the reader, but I think of them now as a crucial means to not reading sacred text badly or even murderously, of reading it well and carefully and alive to context. I thank God for footnotes. And as long as everyone's allowed to speak and nobody bullies anybody, I've yet to meet a Bible study group I didn't like.

Somewhere back there, I was shown that the Bible, as a collection of very different texts canonized as scripture over time, should never be read flatly. As if there is no movement, development, or ethical evolution within the collection itself. The biblical tradition contains traditions within itself that appeal to one another, counter one another, and sometimes leave one another behind. ("You have heard that it was said, but I say to you . . . "; "Do not remember the things of old . . . ") To make the most of it means to hold fast to movement, to receptivity, to new and unforeseen disclosures, to whatever wisdom might arise among us in our contemporary context as we consider its content.

Of the Bible, more than one thing is true. The Bible is a bag of horrors here and there even as it functions, here and there, as a gift to the species. It's also the composition notebook of a centuries-long cara-van of asylum seekers.

IS IT RIGHT FOR YOU TO BE ANGRY?

The communities that gave rise to the biblical witness chronicle their own moral development through the kinds of texts they found some-how essential, even when they had plenty of good reasons for find-ing them embarrassing. When I say that I believe this process and the texts it yields to be inspired, I mean to express my delight and amaze-ment at the inclusion, for instance, of a book like Jonah, famously a deal breaker for many readers given the bit about the man chilling out in the belly of a big fish for three days.

I'm a fan for other reasons.

With four short chapters, this tale—named for its angry and con-fused prophet-protagonist—can be read in under five minutes. We don't find out why until the end, but upon receiving word from on high to go east to Nineveh, capital of Assyria, announcing God's anger against the wickedness of its population, Jonah immediately goes west to board a boat and flee these instructions.

As the story goes, God hurls a wind upon the sea to get Jonah off the ship whose polytheistic crew clearly fears and worships God with more reverence than he does. When they reluctantly deposit him overboard, God commissions an oversized fish to gingerly engulf the prophet and spew him forth on a beach three days later.

Things get weirder.

Now Jonah journeys east and prophesies against Nineveh concern-ing its God-ordained destruction within forty days. With no assur-ance that doing so will win them a reprieve, the Ninevites undertake a mass action of citywide repentance with everyone, from the king to the people to—very strangely—the animals, fasting and donning sackcloth. The cartoonish, extreme lengths to which the inhabitants of Nineveh go in response to the Jewish prophet's word of judgment would be especially outlandish for the story's original audience, for whom Assyrians were held in general contempt. In any case, the God Annihilates Nineveh Tour is canceled.

It is here, within this strange tale, that we receive the sense of why Jonah fled from the Lord at the get-go. He appears to have known, from personal experience, that God had a way of flipping the prophetic script once Jonah had voiced a given oracle. Yet again, the people with a long biblical history of being the objects of God's rage are now subjects of tenderness. God isn't angry, but Jonah is. He falls into a recurrent depression over this familiar pattern of God's moving goalposts. He would rather die than keep being a means of God's loving-kindness to wicked Gentiles.

"Is it right for you to be angry?" God asks Jonah, now witness of the promised destruction he knows will never come. The Socratically delivered object lesson we've seen underway from the beginning continues: God appoints a bush to arise from the ground and provide Jonah with shade, to be followed at sunup by a worm who dutifully destroys the bush, depriving Jonah of relief. God prepares a sultry wind that has Jonah languishing to the point of asking that he be permitted to die.

"Is it right for you to be angry about the bush?" God asks, as if Yoda or Merlin or Stewie Griffin from *Family Guy* is now taunting him a little.

"Angry enough to die," Jonah assures him. And with a bit of rhetoric that concludes the book—we don't hear from Jonah again—God notes that if Jonah is so attached to something as short-lived as a bush, it's at least arguably permissible for God to have a degree of affection for the people of Nineveh and its livestock.

If the divinely appointed worm or the animals in sackcloth aren't enough, the satiric skewering of Jonah on the subject of his own prejudice shows us that what we have here is essentially a *South Park* episode in the middle of the Bible. As a lampooning of a prevalent disposition of many a God-talker, it chronicles a revolutionary realization on the part of its authors concerning who's in and who's out. We can imagine that it probably didn't go over very well initially as it's doubtless something of a minority position that celebrates God's lively refusal to be consistent, to be against the very people some imagined God would be against forever and ever.

But the tradition moved. And the shift, given its inclusion within the collection that came to be called God's Word, is preserved. In this, the short, satiric folktale hits its target, namely those who recognize their own reflection in an angry man comically clinging to a beloved shade bush while resisting the call from on high to value an entire beloved world of people and animals. Who recognize in themselves a man driven to despair over how his conception *of God* is being overturned *by God* yet again.

If we insist, as I once did, that the primary takeaway of the book of Jonah is the need to read every last strange detail (divinely directed fish, bush, worm, winds, etc.) as literal accounts of history, we have yet to enter the psychic struggle at work within it. As someone who once lived in the grip of some catastrophically toxic conceptions of God, myself, and other people, the tale of Jonah hits home. It helps me hold more loosely and compassionately to my own neurotic visions, holding up a mirror to the times I've imagined many (and sometimes most) of my fellow creatures to be not-of-God. The psychic struggle continues.

THE BIBLE TELLS ME SO

When I say I find the Bible inspired, living, active, sharp as any two-edged sword, amazing in the way that it cuts to the heart of all kinds of unexpected issues and invites us to pay attention to ourselves anew, I don't have in mind a single method for reading it in all times and places and seasons of life. I merely speak as a lifelong enthusiast whose sense of curiosity and wonder at the thing deepens with every reading. I find it remarkable and revolutionary that the Jewish community preserved a tale of God's tenderness toward its own enemies alongside prayers for its enemies' painful deaths. When I contemplate the Bible as it comes down to me, it's as if contrary hopes, lines of reasoning, complaints, letters, gospels, lamentations, dream visions, and histories were all squeezed into one space to see what they might produce when taken together, what each might say to the other, what disappointing, wonderful, and unforeseen things might yet come from the mix.

Because it's an ongoing movement, a tale without an ending, trying to rightly contend with something like the Bible is the multifaceted work of generations, a communal labor of many lifetimes. For this reason, to presume to have arrived at the right reading to which anyone else who comes to it will have to submit is bad religion, completely bonkers, and misses the boat entirely. Like Shakespeare, its mysteries live through being received and reenvisioned again and again, differently and better and truer and less nightmarishly. And if the latest listening doesn't challenge to some degree whatever it is I had in mind previously, I can rest assured that I have yet to pay adequate attention.

Needless to say, my account of the ways in which the Bible operates in my existence is not a tale of how we touched and went our separate ways. I'm still reading the mix, taking my own measure by it, to a point, and gratefully not clinging to it quite so nervously or exclusively as my sixteen-year-old self.

The same goes for a defensive posture toward my own identity. Do I identify as someone true to the Bible? A Bible believer? I identify as one who wants to be down in its groove, who received and sought to answer its summons to moral seriousness. This is where witness meets the verdict of others—a community, for instance, or anyone who might observe my behavior and speech and discern a certain process at work, a lived commitment. To make that call for myself is, to my mind, no more appropriate than asserting that I've achieved enlightenment or orthodoxy. There is political power to be accrued by characterizing—marketing—oneself as a person of faith or a proponent, as the best-selling scam has it, of "biblical values," but it's a power that corrupts and compromises a person's spirit, as well as being a rhetorical trick unworthy of morally serious people.

ON THE POSSIBILITY OF BECOMING CHRISTIAN

Whether proffered in an op-ed, in a political campaign, or around the dinner table, it seems to me that a sentence that begins with the words "As a Christian . . . " will usually end badly. What do we hope to gain by speaking this way? If we have in mind, say, a lived pursuit of the ethical path taught and exemplified by Jesus of Nazareth, it's a wonderful adjective that can be rightly—and perhaps righteously—applied to all manner of behavior among all manner of human beings.

It's an aspiration of my own, but to risk deploying it as a plain-as-day self-descriptor is vain, a boast at being an obvious bearer of a wisdom I have yet to deeply receive and live. To presume one's own Christianity, as a mission accomplished, is to place the cart before the horse. I once heard Maya Angelou speak about its being fitting to speak in terms of repeated attempts and lifelong practice: "I'm grateful to be a practicing Christian. I'm always amazed when people say, 'I'm a Christian.' I think, 'Already?' It's an ongoing process. You know, you keep trying. And blowing it and trying and blowing it."[2] Seeking to live up to this wise take on self-identity, I hesitate to call myself a Christian, a Christian convert, *unless* I can be understood to mean I'm not yet done converting to—and learning again what it might mean to convert to—this centuries-long experiment in rightly revering oneself and others sometimes referred to as Christianity.

There are people, a communion of the living and the dead, by whom I'm regularly schooled, nurtured, and renewed. Hardly any of them are Christian in the broadcast-media, self-proclaimed, sound-bite sense, but they all constitute a certain witness that hungers and thirsts for a better-ordered world, an assemblage determined to live lives of social righteousness (not that there's any such thing as a righteousness that *isn't* social). Drawing on the language of what Reverend James Lawson refers to as the nonviolent movement of America, I speak of them as Beloved Community.

And as I experience it, that communion is getting bigger all the time, but one local one with which I identify is a rather small, ragtag congregation of Presbyterians of which I'm pleased to be counted a member. As far as I can tell, I've been largely delivered from the corrosive anxiety that had me ravenously devouring crackers and grape juice in that parking lot, but I'm still eager to dwell along the same trajectory I discerned so dimly as a teenager of a communal pursuit of all things true and beautiful.

In the historical landmark that generally houses this congregation, there are those who, by their own admission, are only there to sing and pray, artists who utilize the space and admire their community's embodied ethic but verbally confess few or none of its creeds, and people who are pleased to have a safe place to discuss and disagree agreeably when we pry open together the real can of worms we called the Bible. I'm pleased to be there as one more pilgrim struggling with the mix of resources that makes up my heritage—that would be my weird religious background—and the blessing and burden of consciousness and conscience it imposes upon me. It should be obvious by now that I can't imagine leaving the tradition into

Theodor Adorno gives a helpfully provocative way of putting it: "One must have tradition in oneself, to hate it properly.

which I was born behind but hope instead to consciously confront it, to occasionally define myself against it, and to somehow dwell faithfully—though not uncritically—within it. That last part inhabits tension. Theodor Adorno gives a helpfully provocative way of putting it: "One must have tradition in oneself, to hate it properly."

Do I hate Christianity? Sometimes. Also, not at all. There's so much to work with. When it isn't genocide or fascism, Christianity is a peasant-philosopher movement deeply in sync with any and every form of Beloved Community. It is, for better or worse, *in* me. My grandfather, the partner of the talkative woman who shamed me as a little child over my Godzilla drawing, was a piece of work who was also a math professor and pastor. If he were alive today, I strongly suspect he might count me among the damned.

And yet he said amazing things. He told my father one time he went hard and heartily to bat for particular doctrines and interpretations of scripture because, after much study and prayer and discussion, he believed that what he had to say was true. *But* in his father-son chat, he cautioned my father that if any part of his examined opinion, any jot or tittle or major theme, ended up being wrong, *move on*. Leave it behind, he said. Do not, under any circumstances, cling to or press forward some backward notion out of love for dear old finite dad. Get disabused as often as possible. Loyalty is not a virtue in itself.

To my knowledge, my grandfather was not familiar with Theodor Adorno or the phrase *critical theory*, and he did not live to hear tell of a form of contemplation called deconstruction. But he seemed to understand that hungering and thirsting after righteousness is a practice as well as a process, a practice best undertaken alongside a steadfast refusal to mistake a position for a person, a cobbled-together idea for a hill to die on, or talk of absolute truth for the thing itself.

A tradition can be a lovely vehicle for loving a self and other selves. But we might have to hate it at least a little before we can love it properly.

STUPEFIED IS A PROCESS

We all have our perceived necessities, our lived commitments. But what I hope to appeal to, within myself and together with others, is a willingness to hold them loosely and with a good-humored eagerness to revise, switch them up, or even abandon them when confronted by witnesses whose experiences differ from our own. *Confronted* can sound dramatic, a little heavy, but I have in mind something positive and even therapeutic.

I've mentioned that the thought of Steve Martin can come to me unexpectedly. He is one of many iconic figures whom I've never met personally but whose witness nevertheless accompanies me. Saying so can sound random, but there's nothing random about it. He is one who, we might say, drew me out at a young age. Anyone who knows me well and knows anything about Steve Martin can confirm that I've purloined from him, my entire life, something of a style, a sound of voice, and, to a degree, a way of imagining the world. At this point, it's more than a little ingrained. I imitate him without thinking about it. Something I realize I do with everyone I admire.

Steve Martin—or the thought of Steve Martin—confronted me in a parking lot as I was trying—by ingesting crackers and grape juice before the strike of midnight—to live a life pleasing to God. His witness helped me hold my own existence, in that moment, and at a slightly different angle. I felt a little silly, but I didn't feel completely stuck or irretrievably stupid. Given what I believed I could discern through his public work, Steve Martin at least finding me interesting and possibly looking upon my strange behavior with curiosity and compassion was

Steve Martin helping me pry something loose within myself. In my parking lot apocalypse, I sometimes felt stupefied by particular ideas about God, myself, and others that I was at risk of shutting down.

I intend *stupefied* here. I believe most everyone experiences a stall, a feeling of shame or stuckness in some context or other. When I sense this grim feeling arising among students, in myself, or on the face of someone I'm observing or myself when we feel out of our depth, denigrated, demeaned, and done with trying to share what we think lest we risk feeling humiliated further, I remind myself and them that I know feelingly that the humility, the process, can be reversed at any time. I've watched it happen. I've felt it happen. I've felt my heart and mind open up again. I've laughed at my own nerviness. I've heard Tom Waits. I've watched people land on an insight, voice it, and sit comfortably and renewed within their own power as they realize and truly take in the fact that someone is listening to them.

Sometimes jumping from that shame, from that stupefied place, is remembering, I'm a fifty-two-year-old white male in Tennessee who attended a segregationist academy for twelve years. It was more than that, but it was at least and devastatingly that. A Confederate soldier was our mascot, and a Confederate flag was our brand. I'm ashamed to say I thought nothing of it. Then I saw Spike Lee's *Do the Right Thing* and Alan Parker's *Mississippi Burning*, and I began to think something much more of it. There was data incoming, and revisions, reappraisals, and adjustments of certain positions became perceived necessities. There is still much to unearth and resist and call out from my weird religious background, which includes a heavy dose of whiteness.

Whiteness is an investment in not knowing (or pretending to not know) things. It is also a commitment to ignore, obscure, or belittle anyone within range who questions the soundness of that investment. It isn't fate. It isn't inevitable. Perhaps one can begin to divest at any time. A lifetime of divestment is in order.

Not unrelatedly, these years of revisioning were also a time I enjoyed listening to the radio personality Rush Limbaugh as I barreled down the highway to get to philosophy class. His brashness, his quick-wittedness, and the apparent ease with which he seemed to make short work of anyone who opposed him energized me. Rush—or the thought of Rush—made me feel strong whenever I felt belittled by history or the eloquence of others. He helped me believe that my anxiety when confronted by the complexity of other people's lives was about *them*, not me. When I was tired of feeling outsmarted, he helped me feel smart again, like an espresso shot of perceived righteousness in myself. In my head, I sometimes had a hard time letting other voices get a word in when he had the microphone.

It goes without saying that he wasn't enough people for me. When confronted by others, including friends less enamored with his ideas than I was, the Rush Limbaugh in my head had to yield. His catechesis was not sufficient for the kind of person I wanted to be. There were better antidotes for my stupefaction, kinder interlocutors all around me, people who believed well of me even when my inner ideologue made noise, when it was painfully obvious that I was letting someone else do my thinking for me. In truth, there was always someone—many someones—holding open a door for me, for the kind of person I wanted to be. Even now, they're all around me.

If I had to offer a definition of sin as I consider my own resistance to feeling shame over where I come from and where I've been, it would be this: sin is active flight from a lived realization of available data. How do I overcome the impulse to deny, to actively avoid knowing what I fear might leave me ashamed or paralyzed or somehow prove to be a personal setback? In the challenge of beholding incoming data and responding righteously to it, we are not without profound, lively, and living resources. In the work of leveling with ourselves and others, we meet a joy, a hope, set before us.

CONTEMPLATING EARTHSEED

Being awake and alive to data is a group activity. We are called to say and share and sing what we see. Others have undertaken this work already, seen and sensed it as the perceived necessity that it is. There are ancient precedents intermingled with current practices. They are sometimes one and the same. Same as it ever was. There are forms of available thoughtfulness here, there, and maybe everywhere.

It is also the case that we are each born into particular infrastructures of bad ideas about ourselves, others, and the natural world. The systems are interlocking and appear indomitable, but they are "only" arrangements. Like any arrangement, they can be challenged and changed. One sense of perceived necessity can overcome another. Patti Smith tells us that we, the people, have the power to wrestle the earth from fools. Hannah Arendt has a lovely word for how this group activity gets started: "Education is the point at which we decide whether we love the world enough to assume responsibility for it and by the same token save it from that ruin which, except for the coming of the new and the young, would be inevitable."[3]

As we love the world enough to say and share and sing what we see, we can honor, revere, and recollect those who preceded us while also nurturing and amplifying the new and the young, without whom there is only ruin. When we do this, we are likely to encounter the conflict that arises in the presence of difference. But without a degree of difference and positive conflict in the meeting of difference, the mixed feelings that put a kind of stress upon the mind, we can't grow.

Difference is the sunshine. When there is no difference, there is no relationship, nothing to work with or build upon, no creative friction with which to make fun, seek to understand, or stumble into the promise of drama. No way to get into it with one another. Without difference, there's nothing to get and keep the ball rolling and the data incoming. Nothing much to love.

Art Spiegelman, author of *Maus*, likes to get into it. He knows the power of a runaway train of thought *and* the collective effort, among easily frightened people, to control it. The attempt to control speech is, perhaps more often than not, the attempt to control thought. Here's how Spiegelman once described his own sense of perceived necessity: "The answer to speech, in my religion, is more speech, a lot of yakking—and a lot of drawing."⁴

I love the provocation and the sense of play here. It's perfectly harmless, but, depending on the fear level of those present, the freedom to yak and draw Spiegelman sees as essential (and also essential to the faith that informs him) can feel threatening and even dangerous. It's a sacred freedom—but it isn't welcome, acceptable, or even legal in many contexts. I see Spiegelman's summons to impassioned, creative discourse as a call to love my own life enough to risk bringing it to expression in the company of others, to love the world enough to say and sing and draw and act out what I think I'm seeing. This, too, is a way of getting unstuck, unstupefied, and righteously responsive (rather than reactive) to incoming data.

Education, in this sense, is the slow, steady, but also sometimes sudden overcoming of deferential fear. Many of us are taught to defer, to keep our heads down, and to know our place. We're often made to feel afraid to think for ourselves. It is precisely being in these places that can inspire a risky word or joke or breakthrough laughter, sometimes coming from us, sometimes others. We draw our courage where we can.

"Shyness is shit. It isn't cute or feminine or appealing. It's torment, and it's shit." This is the Afro-futurist writer Octavia Butler describing the challenge of overcoming her own deferential fear. I look to her regularly to overcome my own, and I share her work and her witness in an effort to extend the gift she's been to me. In the classroom, when those words ("Shyness is shit") are read and discussed aloud among students, I feel something shift. I believe a kind of permission is getting handed over. Someone's said what something hard to say is like. A door is getting held open.

Like no other writer I know of, Octavia Butler gives us language for thinking about our own creative intuition in relation to other individuals' creative intuition. When she speaks of shyness, I understand that she's describing a fear-driven disinclination to in part pay heed to one's own creative intuition. Like avoiding or fleeing a lived realization of available data, this shyness can become a form of estrangement from your own best, liveliest, most responsive self. When succumbed to fully, shyness, she tells us, is torment, a form of death in life. The alternative to shyness is genuine self-advocacy, true devotion to your own creative intuition, which she terms "positive obsession." Listen:

> *Obsession can be a useful tool if it's positive obsession. Using it is like aiming carefully in archery. . . . I saw positive obsession as a way of aiming yourself, your life, at your chosen target. Decide what you want. Aim high. Go for it. . . . Positive obsession is about not being able to stop just because you're afraid and full of doubts. Positive obsession is dangerous. It's about not being able to stop at all.[5]*

Positive obsession would go on to be an essential practice within Earthseed, the sacred tradition discovered, stumbled upon, refined, and developed by Lauren Oya Olamina, the teenage narrator-protagonist of Butler's novel *Parable of the Sower*. Chronicling the survival of a community she forms in the year 2024 within what remains of North America following slow and steady climate catastrophe hastened by an authoritarian political party controlled by foreign interests, the story is also a series of dialogues about Lauren's homegrown religion, whether it's ultimately of any use at all, and what it is, exactly, she's asking of the people who come to loosely adhere to her teachings. As you might imagine, it's all eerily prescient and eye-rubbingly relevant to where we find ourselves in the here and now.

If the Parable of the Sower attributed to Jesus of Nazareth can be thought of as a theory of culture, a contemplative tale offering food for thought on what becomes of people and ideas given their very different contexts (different soils), which can involve withering away, getting eaten up, or, with sufficient moisture, thriving and bearing fruit, Butler's novel is further contemplation on and beyond Jesus's contemplation. Lauren follows Marx's dictum ("the critique of religion is the prerequisite of every critique") by letting her interlocutors shape her own read on her own studied but also impromptu ideas. In one exchange, she notes the practical benefit of praying to God but bristles at the suggestion that Earthseed has any investment at all in unexamined worship: "Earthseed deals with ongoing reality, not with supernatural authority figures. Worship is no good without action. With action, it's only useful if it steadies you, focuses your efforts, eases your mind."[6]

While an appeal to divine transcendence, a harmonious future, and loving self and others well is at the core of Earthseed, Lauren never claims that her insights aren't available to anyone and everyone who expends the effort of paying attention. In this, Earthseed is a consciously communal form of positive obsession: "I wish I could believe that it was all supernatural, and that I'm getting messages from God. But then, I don't believe in that kind of God. All I do is observe and take notes, trying to put things down in ways that are as powerful, as simple, and as direct as I feel them."[7] Please note the resonance here with Art Spiegelman's relentless commitment to better analogies, drawings, and ways of putting it. Earthseed is also meaningfully in sync with James Joyce's hope that he could somehow discern, serve, and help sustain "a more veritably human tradition"[8] with courage, candor, and conscience.

In *Parable of the Sower*, Octavia Butler takes up a similar task by offering a way of cherishing forms of faith while also refusing to succumb to dogmatism. Lauren frequently declines to view Earthseed as a novel form or a peculiarly innovative turn in human history. She describes other characters, even those possessed by catastrophically toxic ideas about self, God, and others, as fellow pilgrims who've also "assembled"[9] their conception of self, others, and divinity out of that which has traditioned its way down to them for better and worse. Butler provides a way of envisioning sacred tradition—*any* sacred tradition—as a mixed bag, or many mixed bags, out of which we draw and make choices.

Earthseed is one way of naming and describing the process many of us are caught up in as we decide what to make of our own inheritance.

What do we keep?

What do we cling to?

What do we want within our bandwidth, our headspace, our quiver of essential intelligence?

What do we need to rid ourselves of if we hope to access moral adulthood?

Butler herself, though not identifying as religious, had an appreciative word for the faith of her childhood: "I'm glad I was raised as a Baptist, because I got my conscience installed early. I've been around people who don't have one, and they're damned scary."[10]

Something of this posture is evident in *Parable of the Sower* as Lauren is getting to know a beautiful man named Bankole. Asking him about his religion, he notes that he doesn't exactly have one: "When my wife was alive, we went to a Methodist church. Her religion was important to her, so I went along. I saw how it comforted her, and I wanted to believe, but I never could."

Lauren notes that, while raised Baptist, she's in a similar boat: "I couldn't make myself believe either, and I couldn't tell anyone.

My father was the minister. I kept quiet and began to understand Earthseed."

"Began to invent Earthseed," Bankole interjects.

This is where Lauren offers a beautifully nuanced take on what occurs when we thoughtfully take up—and, if necessary, put to the side or drop altogether—the stories, images, lyrics, and sayings that serve our human thriving, the available lore, if you like, of a given time and place. It isn't invention exactly. "Began to discover and understand it. Stumbling across the truth isn't the same as making things up." Earthseed, she explains, is about discovering and acting upon "the essentials,"[11] which will always differ between people, experiences, soils, and other contexts.

Here's a little adage for the believer in Earthseed: whatever lore helps you love yourself and others more is lore enough.

The task, I suspect, in juggling all of this while remaining open to—rather than reactive against—incoming data is to be lively and responsive agents of

Whatever lore helps you love yourself and others more is lore enough.

our own recollections. By doing so, we practice positive obsession, a healthy form of religion that doesn't involve degrading or debasing ourselves but, instead, cooperating with our most creative, intuitive selves.

This brings us back to the poetic, prophetic intelligence of the heart's affections. Earthseed recognizes the depth and dignity of our individual experience while registering the creative labor of those who came before us. Where we stand determines what we see, but there's something singular and sacred in our own situatedness, the minute particularities of any one person's vision. And if the heart is half prophet, each person's visionary perspective has the potential to enrich anyone and everyone else's.

In this sense, Earthseed partners nicely with William Blake's celebration of the human form divine—that's every human being who's ever lived—as holy, as a bearer of infinite value. Both are a relentlessly social vision of profound hospitality *and* profound self-respect, of conceiving self and others as conduits of wisdom and essential insight.

Both are also a helpful corrective to the crushing of spirits, the religious trauma that marks so many who share backgrounds like mine, and the toxic speech and behaviors that arise when that trauma's never acknowledged, talked about, or dealt with. Blake claimed to discern "mind-forged manacles" among those who are burdened, laid low, and estranged from the prophet within.

Like Butler, Blake was well acquainted with the doctrines and ideologies, still persisting among us, that escalate despair and self-hatred. And like Butler, he had lively responses to every bad idea that came his way. "Honest Indignation is the Voice of God," he insisted. What a way of revering every honest word that breaks into our bandwidth. What a way of keeping the doors of perception open to Earthseed, to hearing, receiving, and being it.

There's a related anecdote that performs a similar function. It comes to us through Crabb Robinson, who once visited Blake and put certain questions to him in December 1825: "On my asking in what light he viewed the great question concerning the Divinity of Jesus Christ, he said; '*He is the only God.*' But then he added—'And so am I and so are you.'"[12]

I confess I love this. It overcomes a sometimes deadly dualism most helpfully and can inspire a sense of due reverence in our consideration of family, friends, and ideological opponents if we'll let it. Paying heed, heartily and humbly, to what we love and why, to what others love and why, is a holy work. To love a person is to love a process. To love a self is to love a process. What might it mean to begin to see what we've seen?

2

ATTENTION COLLECTION

Art happens in an act of attention.

—Guy Davenport

I was a junior in high school when I first beheld the cover of Peter Case's first solo album in the pages of *Rolling Stone*. He was seated at a table full of black-and-white composition notebooks and harmonicas. He looked kind and affable and a little bit like me. I was ready to love whatever it was he had to sing and say long before I procured the cassette. Once I did, I was sold, and I urged his work—folk rock is what we called it at the time—on anyone who was willing to sit still for it. He was up there with Tom Waits and Elvis Costello for me. Models for getting set free. Avenues for accessing Earthseed, the cosmic plainspeak, that which expands the space of the talkaboutable, the available lore for loving ourselves and others more.

In time, I met him at a show, and over the years, we've communicated a little, talking William Blake and Shakespeare and the end of the world. Years ago, I watched him lead a discussion among young aspiring musicians concerning lifelong habits of creativity. He talked about how the artist operates as a thieving magpie, always on the lookout for bits, threads, and fragments that might serve in the assembling of a nest in which to live, look, and give form to the inner situation. With the same working survival instinct, the artist draws inspiration from a half-remembered remark, a billboard, an odd facial expression misperceived, a snatch of dialogue among strangers, or whatever's at hand—sometimes directly or word for word—to articulate something needful, new, and timely whether in lyric, image, story, or argument.

> **We are, each of us, libraries full of experience, sensations, words spoken for and against us, memories of joy and trauma, inexplicable scenes, and unresolved stories. What insight might await us when we attempt to articulate it a little.**

"How old are you guys?" he asked when a lull had set in. Most reported themselves to be in their late teens and early twenties. Nodding, he surprised everyone by saying, "You've seen enough then. You have more than enough material to get you where you're going." After a pause, "But maybe you haven't *seen* what you've seen."

Maybe you haven't *seen* what you've seen.

What a line. And like a good magpie, I went ahead and made that one my own, repeating it as often as possible, the better to take the admonition to heart and broadcast the call to fuller consciousness whenever occasions permit. And what an essential burden to make sure you're still taking on this business of being awake to yourself—to be a witness to your own experience, to listen to your own life, to see what you've seen. Art, after all, is how we become aware of ourselves, and it's *for* everyone. What could be more essential, more sacred, more religious, more holy? After all, nobody can do the work of being true for you.

The mysterious alchemy of learning—of awakening to ourselves—happens, and the least we can do is say so, letting people know when they've helped us along, when they've somehow visualized, lyricized, or said something that was in our heads. We get to testify concerning the how and the why of it, and I'm not sure we're quite alive to ourselves till we've begun to do so. With this in mind, every writing class I've taught—or presumed to try to teach—has begun with some variation of the question of how we might best go about *seeing* what we've seen. We are, each of us, libraries full of experience, sensations, words spoken for and against us, memories of joy and trauma, inexplicable scenes, and unresolved stories. What insight might await us when we attempt to articulate it a little, when we begin to open up the book of what all's happened?

KING KONG BURGER

Marshall McLuhan tells us that when we distinguish entertainment from education we only demonstrate that we don't understand the first thing about either, and if religion names our perceived necessities, the work of being awake and alive to what we're up to requires thinking hard and honestly about the instruction we've received and internalized, what we've found ourselves abiding. We become what we abide. How is it, precisely, that we've been proselytized? Religion is in the details.

One early, formative memory of my own—as vivid as any Sunday school lesson—goes back to the time the Wendy's corporation (the Nashville franchise, anyway) once made life peculiarly difficult for my mother. At the age of six, I'd seen King Kong standing atop the World Trade Center with a flaming aircraft in one hand and a scantily clad Jessica Lange in the other, and somehow I knew he understood. It wouldn't be too long before I'd proudly sport the image on a metal lunchbox. But in those days of more primitive-feeling affiliations between the fast-food industry and the emerging phenomenon of blockbuster films, Wendy's had me at hello when they advertised their King Kong Burger. The very name of the thing was enough to set me imagining any number of Kong-related products: a doll, a badge, a mask, or even a figurine beneath the bun covered in ketchup and mustard. A true believer in Kong, I took them at their word. I needed to get to the nearest Wendy's without delay. My mother had seen the commercial and knew this trail of supposed associations to be a dead end, but my heart was set, so she saw fit to facilitate the learning moment. She would show me what a King Kong Burger had to do with the King. We went, she paid up, and we sat at a table together as I stared at the lumpen mess so utterly void of Kong. No semblance of Kong even on the wrapper. *In name only*, legally and literally, as advertised. The name, I was made to see and know in my heart and nervous system, was a false witness. An unhappy meal. No satisfaction. Mostly a minimalist when it came to burgers, I couldn't even eat the thing. The con was on, and it went way beyond Kong. She held my hand through the heartbreak.

The six-year-old would not have put it this way, but I'd received difficult instruction concerning the way advertised realities could so easily mess with my own longing for a world made richer by the likes of King Kong. And blessedly, given the love and the care that accompanied such well-orchestrated realizations, I was never made to feel ashamed of my reaching after that illusory something. Many Micronauts, Star Wars action figures, and a slew of comic books would be demanded and provided in the years to come, but this particular epiphany would linger and take on the referential powers of a household anecdote. There are, after all, so many King Kong equivalents at every stage of human development as well as many a moment when the promise of a richer world hoped for comes true.

I remember feeling I'd begun to offer something back in these exchanges the day I read *Watership Down* aloud to my mother on a long car trip. She was a captive audience, but I could tell she was really getting into it, visibly enjoying my enjoyment to the point that I felt it was hers too. It was finally happening; I heard and knew myself as a convincing teller of tales. Something stuck.

CATECHISM FOR THE DAY

Both of these episodes made it into my quiver of essentials because they're points along a trajectory without which I can't begin to explain myself to myself. I think, too, of the time a quiet and charmingly broody young woman in a high-school art class saw fit to bestow upon me a mixtape of Suzanne Vega songs. Was it something I said? What had I done to indicate I was possibly a kindred spirit? The fact is I'm still trying to live up to this gesture, this vote of confidence that I might be, or prove to be, someone alive to what she sensed in Suzanne Vega. By crediting me in this way, she'd propelled me into a life more interesting.

"Tell me what you like and I'll tell you what you are," the Victorian-era art critic John Ruskin once decreed. This strikes me as both alarming and entirely true. What do I like and why? Really thinking that one through is as intensely telling as it is to genuinely try to answer that profound question "What are you into?" I'd have to begin with my attention collection, my book of common things, my working palette of lifelong recognitions.

Looking at it honestly is a way of taking stock of the way my imagination's been formed and my behavior shaped, a chronicling of all that's somehow inspired confidence or a feeling of orienting knowingness within me. I'm also immediately reminded how unceasingly communal this process is. Literacy occurs between people, and it spreads one reading recommendation, one "You should check this out," one "I thought of you," and one playlist at a time. I've been the glad recipient, repeatedly, of myriad acts of intellectual hospitality on the part of people who've been kind enough to see within me an intelligence I had yet to access myself, people who saw fit to take me seriously by regarding me hopefully and imaginatively. Maybe you have been too.

Given my frightened and lonely reading of the Bible—a common occurrence in the place that I come from—I was in serious need of such hospitality. I remember feeling weirdly elated by the fact of Robert De Niro reading 1 Corinthians 13 aloud in *The Mission*. It was as if one world was allowed to draw on another. Maybe it happened all the time. Maybe it was all one world. A damaging division, artificial as it was, was casually overcome by one more little pebble landing inside the wall I was in danger of building around myself, and I held on to it for dear life. I'd hear biblical references in Peter Gabriel and A-ha lyrics. One source could speak to another as I spied a way to open my circle of affirmation a tiny bit to include more forms of human solidarity. I believe this is how the good work gets done. I've been delivered from certain madness by certain loves. What I love are poetry and gospel—not that there's a tremendous difference between the two.

And they're everywhere, these means whereby we begin to see what we're seeing. That which was unnamed gets suddenly put into words. That heavy happening never justly described or illuminated in our hearing finally receives fresh articulation and gets brought into the light of clear expression. A breakthrough occurs. It's what Shakespeare describes as imagination bodying forth the form of things heretofore unknown, conferring upon them tangible shapes and conjuring out of what used to be an airy, oft-debilitating nothing, a local habitation and a name, a way of putting it.

To speak of one beloved format, this is the hope of the paleo-playlist, mixtape tradition, an early experience of mine in the giving, receiving, and trading of attention collections. "Here's a little something that orders my existence," we might say as we hand our enthusiasms over. It's a more time-consuming and tactile procedure than we're lately accustomed to in our age of social recommendation, where a "like" or a tweet or an article posted online seems to sink to the bottom of the oceans of internet within seconds, but it's the same communal impulse.

Sharing what we're up to—what we believe we're discovering—with others is what stewards the possibility of friendship and revelation. It's the handing down and over—that's tradition—of what sacred intuition we hope we've accessed, the Earthseed of it all. How else do we access the meaning of our own experience? How else do we see what we've seen?

We're always being catechized in one way or another, and figuring out how the process has gone so far and might yet go is the lifetime work of critical consciousness. To look hard at our attention collections—what's in there and why?—is to undertake the ancient imperative of the Delphic motto: know thyself.

Is this a task we still feel we can afford?

Are people still up for doing this kind of thing?

What kind of role do we want to have in our own daily catechesis?

I WAS RAISED CAPITALIST

In the song and dance I undertake as my teaching routine, I often suspect my primary duty is to alert students to the fact they've been catechized at all, that their cultural formation is a living fact long underway as opposed to a phenomenon they can successfully get clear of and gaze upon with an air of detachment.

It befalls me to invite my students to begin to conceive religion, against popular wisdom, as a notion that might possibly apply to their own lives as easily as it does to those who haven't made it this far in their supposed education. When they enter a university classroom, they have reason to believe that they're expected to leave the worrisome details of their particular religious backgrounds at the door lest they risk being perceived as narrow, backward, or hopelessly biased. They're almost painfully well-catechized in the move so many in the westernizing world make these days: *I'm not religious.* It can be exceedingly difficult to discuss religion with people absolutely certain that only other people have been in contact with one.

"If religion is our subject, we'll have a much better time together," I observe to them, "and we'll have *a lot* more to talk about if we're willing to dare a little vulnerability and at least a smidgen of transparency concerning . . . would it help if we called it religious *baggage*? Are there ideas in and by which we were reared that we find it hard to—or even feel we mustn't—let go? Let's not be stingy in sharing them. Let's have a go at being openhanded." First written assignment? Describe *your* weird religious background.

"We all have one," I argue. "I'd be willing to bet many of you were probably raised capitalist, for instance." This somehow signals a clearing of the air. If we're going to deploy the idea of religion for all it's worth, we'll have to put everything on the table. We won't limit ourselves to talk about divinity or strange opinions concerning life after death; we're talking what's been normalized, learned behaviors and social formations, the shape of our enthusiasms, the ways we order our worlds, what we're hoping for in everything we're up to, and the prickly question of what it is we genuinely decree essential—basically, the alarming realization of what we're really up to, that dramatic fact that rises to the surface in each of us for all to see, slowly and surely, a few days into the zombie apocalypse.

But the big reveal—*apocalypsis* is just Greek for "revelation"—of how it is we've been *informed*, what it is that constitutes our perceived necessities, need not await the appearance among us of the walking dead. We can begin to think about that one now. I have in mind here the amazing aphorism—perhaps worthy of a tattoo—dropped upon us by Albert Camus by way of his narrator, Jean-Baptiste Clamence, in his novel *The Fall*: "I'll tell you a big secret, *mon cher*. Don't wait for the Last Judgment. It takes place every day."[1]

Game on. Why not take a look at what we're into, those patterns of behavior we're often immersed in so thoroughly and hypnotically that we have to fight for the right to even think about them? Let's look hard together. We're welcome to say whatever we want to about all the things we believe, but any sacred tradition we care to reference will remind us that the surest evidence of what we believe is what we do.

Game on. Why not take a look at what we're into, those patterns of behavior we're often immersed in so thoroughly and hypnotically?

Faith without works is . . . not actually your faith, as it turns out. We do what we believe—maybe it's a relief to even say it aloud—and we *don't* do what we don't. It's no secret after all.

If what I believe is what I say and do, the guiding provocation runs like this: show me your receipts, your text messages, your gas mileage, your online history, a record of your daily doings, and, just to get things started, a transcript of the words you've spoken aloud in the course of a single day, and *then* we might begin to get a picture of your perceived necessities.

What doors of perception might begin to open when we allow ourselves to look at religion—and our own lives—in this way?

What personal hypocrisies do many of us keep obscured to ourselves when we don't?

The living witness of what we do with our lives speaks even as it writes out our detailed histories, and it doesn't operate according to all those ultimately unsustainable compartmentalizations we use to fool ourselves and others. No blind trusts, we might say, in the playing out of my religion.

I BELIEVE RADIOHEAD

But we begin with attention collections. There's no sacred tradition apart from some form of canonization. So why not begin considering the question of religion by way of our own personal canons? Every class is an opportunity to, in some sense, simultaneously present my attention collection to students each day (I already wanted to do that anyway) and to urge them to become more alertly appreciative and aware of their own. We all have them—I manage to keep myself from shouting—these lines, memories, advertisements, shows, songs, and scenarios we go to instinctively because we find them convincing, meaningful, comforting, and maybe somehow clarifying. And there's a reason—so many reasons—they're there. Let's explore them. Let's have a go at sharing the intelligence we've gathered. As long as we're here, let's somehow expand the space of the talkaboutable together.

Inevitably, I detect resistance, so I begin to show my hand. I like Radiohead. Or to put it more specifically, I *believe* Radiohead. In truth, I'm persuaded by them. Their take on the world enriches my own, making me more alive to myself and others, more attentive to what William Blake calls the minute particulars, the oft-overlooked, on-the-ground details that make up the lives we lead. Anyone who hopes to do good to another person, according to Blake, will have to attend to—"labour well"—the minute particulars, minutely particularizing their so-called love. Radiohead is an ever-present help in the trouble I meet when I try my hand at the work of loving well by loving specifically. They call upon me—perhaps you can hear the call too—to immerse *my soul* in love. Radiohead. I drink their Kool-Aid.

As it turns out, not every college student feels the love for Radiohead, but testifying unrestrainedly serves to prepare a table of expectation in the wilderness. We're going to attempt to be present to one another by owning aloud our own interests and enthusiasms, reflecting on the art that, in Franz Kafka's phrase, is (or was) the ice ax striking at the frozen sea inside us. What voices somehow get through and why? It's often a tall order for most, but it's also an invitation to become more deeply aware of what's going on in our minds, to take ourselves more seriously, and, most important, to feel our own worth. Holding out an artifact or two from our attention collections is a very good place to start.

A river of hypocrisy and denial probably runs through it, but my attention collection covers a lot of territory: R.E.M., Chance the Rapper, Aretha Franklin singing "R-E-S-P-E-C-T," *Midnight Mass*, Alan Moore's *Watchmen*, Toni Cade Bambara, *Twin Peaks*, Fanny Howe, U2, Laurie Anderson, all manner of human goodness. I take these witnesses to heart and, in no small way, measure my life by them. I'd be squandering the gift of consciousness they give me were I to keep it all to myself, hiding it under a bushel, as it were, getting lost in my hopeless little screen. What good is a revelation if we refuse to offer witness? Who wants to laugh or shake a fist at injustice or experience an insight all by themselves?

The job is to amplify the oracle always. I collect and share what I feel I've been given in the way of illumination. I find myself compiling, tweaking, amending, and constantly reconfiguring. It's a process we're all up to in one way or another. It's a mental journal to help us wake up from the hypnosis we know to be possible and even likely in the sometimes weary world too often prone to tantrums. And in this sense, attention collections might be our primary way of being social, of having something hopeful to give people when we happen upon them, something that might somehow overcome whatever initially appears to divide us from one another.

BRING FORTH WHAT IS WITHIN YOU

I presume this is the kind of task Jack Kerouac had in mind when he expressed his desire to be a great rememberer, someone who manages, from time to time, to redeem life from darkness by remembering well, by remembering people, places, and experiences truly, wholly, and holily. Broad is the path of *dis*membering, and narrow is the gate of righteous remembering. But there remains the duty to chronicle the life and liveliness we witness in the hope of preserving and passing on visions that sustain despite the reigning distortions, visions that hold everything dear. We know the fear-driven pressure to reduce, to control, and to cut everything and everyone down to manageable size. This, too, is religion, nightmare religion, and its calls to worship are everywhere. But true religion, remembering well amid the haste, hurry, and distraction of the average day, requires a conscious effort. Being an ecstatic affirmer, a noticer supreme, is a full-time job.

Such remembering is anything but a turning away from the world; it's the servicing and handing on of visions that lend our lives coherence against that which degrades and destroys. What Kerouac means to heed himself and issue to all within earshot is the call to creative literacy, that conscientious communality of which we're all capable, the call to steward our own experience, to not be indifferently absorbed in our own lives, the sweet burden of thinking socially, the Earthseed of it all.

Kerouac wasn't the first to have a go at being a poet-prophet. There's a long history of trying to be one more person upon whom very little is lost. Most are anonymous, but they hold the world carefully in their generous hands. We might say all are called, in some way, to keep the faith by way of intense attentiveness. As accounts of the Beat Generation's history have it, Allen Ginsberg once handed an early attempt at a poem to Kerouac, who read it delightedly, observing, "See? You can do it too."

This is the form that *taking care* takes. And we can't really do it with our arms folded tight. It's the generosity upon which the human species depends, and as an unendingly communal activity, it always and ever requires a village. As the food critic voiced by Peter O'Toole (aptly named Anton Ego) in *Ratatouille* wisely and humbly observes in wide-awake awareness of his own inescapably social vocation, "The new needs friends."

If we're beginning to accept the work of always cultivating our attention collections with care as a kind of cultural obligation, I'd like to push the notion further by observing that it might be more helpfully held as a sacred necessity, a pursuit of the holy. If I'm not in the habit of consciously exercising my own imagination, there are armies of con artists with many a King Kong equivalent who are more than willing to do it for me, to capitalize on my neuroses at every turn. If I'm not careful, I could find myself storming the Capitol, imagining I'm somehow loving God.

The barricaded mind is a dangerous one. A saying attributed to Jesus in the Gospel of Thomas puts the matter starkly: "If you bring forth what is within you, what you bring forth will save you. If you do not bring forth what is within you, what you do not bring forth will destroy you."[2] Or as Steve Earle once put it to that endlessly beleaguered soul named Bubbles on *The Wire*, "You gotta let it out to let it go."

THE MIRACLE OF ATTENTIVENESS

In this sense, the act of self-expression, putting our stories, our jams, our beloved enthusiasms on the table, isn't just an essential practice of self-preservation; it also creates the possibility of neighborliness, a meaning-making exercise in the work of being a human being among human beings. In my own stumbling efforts to draw my children into a wakefulness of hearing, sharing, and carefully following the stories that surround us, I was once schooled by my son, Sam, who'd skipped straight to an insight I had yet to reach: "So literacy is about cooperating with people?"

Undoubtedly. It's the most joyous game in town. In the long haul, literacy is a lifelong practice of attentiveness, of really believing in the strange actuality of other humans whose lives might speak persuasively and blessedly into your own. As Guy Davenport reminds us, our attention collections are the stomping grounds of art: "Art happens in an act of attention . . . that is to be transferred, after being made into an intelligible shape, to other minds. We forget that this is a miracle."

This is the joy of experiencing our own lives and those of others without defensiveness, to see and say what we're haunted by, what we cherish, and why. True religion requires it. It's a group activity. If we deny or repress our attention collections, hiding them away from the bright light of day, we diminish ourselves and likely anyone who might dare to try to be in relationship with us in our guarded, toxic states.

But if we value what we're up to and into enough to celebrate and share it, we're no longer closed off to the genius of others, and our isolation is overcome by the heartening presence of other people. The more we share what we're into with candor and openness while inviting and allowing other people to return the favor, really receiving the input we've perhaps been secretly hoping for all along, the richer and more varied our attention collections become.

Which is why that richness calls for us to hold our collections out to one another with open hands. We get to share and reflect upon our source materials together. I wouldn't have much of one to begin with without the gifts, the urgings, the recommendations, the unconscious instruction of so many. "I think you might like this" is my love language. It's an indication that someone's given thought to the shape of my affections to imagine they've found something they suspect might speak to me. It also means they've gone ahead and loved something enough to get a little preachy about it. I'm always looking for a word of inspiration, a better take on reality.

Who doesn't want *that*? Who *isn't* running down a dream and hoping it might lead to a better vision for inhabiting the world hopefully? Well, it's complicated. We have ever before us so many false witnesses to sift out from the true, so many schemes that prey on the reigning disorientation many of us feel most of the time, so many fake signals mixed in among the authentic and therefore revelatory witnesses. Nevertheless, the miracle of attentiveness is passed down and handed over and bandied about one poem, one podcast, one Bible study, one book club at a time. Earthseed is what there is.

"I think you might like this" is my love language.

But we have to show up for these things. We have to contemplate the film or the album before forming a judgment on it. We have to read to the bottom of the article. We have to see the witness, get the drift, before we can begin to reject or receive it. Discerning, processing, and passing on the gift of attentiveness takes time. If a tradition is a never-ending hand-me-down, we have to sit still and even meditate a little to figure out what enriches, what needs to be rejected, or what we'll do well to rethink a little. In the case of any story or song, it will take time to see clearly and actually witness what particular people were trying to hand down in their own context *then* before we can begin to experience what there is to meaningfully hand down *now*. Real affection will involve investment and follow-up. It might not even feel like work. It's best understood and undertaken as a form of joy.

And again, conscious cultivation of our own thought life is a sacred necessity, nothing less than a determined involvement in our own Earthseed, our own perceived necessity. Why not be conscious participants in our own catechesis? The catechesis is happening whether we choose to engage it or not, and as ever, we're alarmingly free to look hard at any time at what we've learned, what we're learning, and what we might do well to unlearn. What's been normalized—woefully or beautifully—and why? Are there untapped resources for being transformed by the ongoing renewal of our minds instead of being led around by fear and anxiety and the everyday denials that accompany them? What choices might deeper consciousness require?

There are opportunities for joy, insight, and embodiment here. Be the Earthseed you want to see in the world.

3

CHOOSE YOUR ANCESTORS CAREFULLY

It's hard to overstate how deep the need can get for things to make sense.

—Sean Phillips in John Darnielle's *Wolf in White Van*

A remarkable and disturbing *Saturday Night Live* skit from the twentieth century often comes to my mind as a treasured touchstone in my attention collection. I've found I somehow can't get over it. It features Will Ferrell most prominently as he harnesses that sense of raw human madness he snaps into like nobody else. As I measure these things, it achieves a degree of comedic perfection, prophetic in its way, as it lampoons and even revels in the fracturing of an alleged orderliness upon which social relations seem to depend. What happens when the given script of what's appropriate is suddenly unavailable? What will we do with ourselves?

It's the carefully scripted celebration of the twentieth-anniversary episode of a Phoenix-based morning show called *Wake Up and Smile*.[1] As the opening theme song fades, Ferrell and his coanchor, played by

Nancy Walls, get the show underway and exchange pleasantries with David Alan Grier as the friendly weatherman. They laugh and smile and agree that their decades-long work together "has *definitely* been a fun ride." But the transition into the cooking tips portion of the show is suddenly interrupted by the failure of essential technology, or, as Ferrell's man-in-charge puts it, "The teleprompter . . . on which everything we say appears on . . . is broken. . . . We're having what is known in the business as . . . technical times." Amid a dawning sense of panic and heavy breathing, Ferrell and Walls are urged by those behind the camera to undertake the impossibly unexpected labor of ad-libbing.

"You know . . . " Ferrell begins with a blank, anxious stare into his own inner resources. "I had a notion the other day."

"Well," Walls responds approvingly. "Um . . . notions make this country . . . happen."

What notion arises from Ferrell's raw feed? "I . . . I was thinking someone should get a group together . . . with guns to sweep out those ghettos." And before he can take the words back, we cut to a commercial break. Something has risen to the surface. Sounds about white.

Upon returning, the hosts are holding their positions, looking around helplessly, clutching their armrests and spouting off inanities arising from deep within their hearts. Walls: "I . . . drive a red car." Ferrell: "Make sure those poor people stay away from it. They've got swords." Grier: "Fear. I must control the fear. Please. *Someone tell me what to say.*"

Nervously taking up the mantle of "the dominant one," Ferrell flails in the direction of what he believes their situation must require: "Easy . . . Easy. If we panic, we die! . . . We must use the furniture to build a barricade." Taking apart the set to defend against every imagined threat—his coanchor's barely articulate complaints of feeling cold, hungry, and alone ("There's no words!") and the weatherman's desperate pleas to an unknown "They" who, if they all wait patiently, might see fit to *give back the words*—Ferrell lets out an agonized scream abruptly cut off by another commercial.

It's even more downhill from there, and it goes—alarmingly—over the top. Their minutes of lawlessness yield torches, a beheading, a turtle on loan from the zoo they're now determined to consume for nourishment, and a shirtless Will Ferrell with a black handprint on his chest loudly decreeing, "The order of the hand will rule!" And just as gore and chaos have conquered all hope of restoration, the teleprompter is online again, *the words have returned,* and our presenters are expected to snap back to their trusty old composed routine. Through blood, sweat, and tears of anguish and gratitude, our hosts try to deflect attention from the horror they've wrought while unscripted as they try to find their way back to their previously in-progress celebration, under dictation, of "twenty magical years of *Wake Up and Smile.*"

I'm not entirely sure why this skit delights me so. What is it that thrills me in this catastrophic kerfuffle, the grand façade so soon burning, the rapid dissolution of a late-'90s social contract? Why has it lingered after all these years? Do I really imagine this particular live footage of late-night song and dance is, in some deep sense, somehow telling the truth?

I'll readily admit that I do. When I find myself sitting quietly and nodding knowingly among a group of people being addressed—or trying to appear as if they're being addressed—by someone else, I often hear the words of the great and powerful Oz arising ineluctably in my mind: "Pay no attention to the man behind the curtain." I believe great evil is normalized and obscured in every area of our public life. I worry over what forms of conscience, soul, and liveliness are suppressed and somehow evaded when things are expected to take a turn for the formal. I wonder what

I believe great evil is normalized and obscured in every area of our public life.

spirit is made to flee—and what different spirit is made to enter in—when we clear our throats to signal that *now* we're getting down to business. What transition do we *think* we're staging? What did we leave behind, and where are we supposedly going in the guise of our somehow suddenly serious—as if by magic—selves? Who are we kidding?

THE SOCIAL PIPELINE

This twenty-year-old skit poses the crucial question of where we really are apart from the social cues, prompts, and stage directions by which we figure out how to assure one another we can be trusted, reasoned with, and counted on to not behave like sociopaths, not to try to overturn, for instance, the results of a presidential election. It makes comically plain our desperate desire to know what it is we're supposed to be doing, but . . . what if that's *all* we're doing? What if, like Tolstoy's *The Death of Ivan Ilyich*, our lifelong commitment to discerning and performing what's *considered* to be socially acceptable is precisely where we're stalled in our development, never seriously asking the essential question of whether what's *expected* of us in our day-to-day existence is what's right? What if that which is celebrated, championed, and praised in our particular milieu is, as it turns out, an all-pervading social darkness we've come to accept and look to as light? Perhaps we're interested in finding out. Maybe we've met some people who appear to be interested in such questions. Maybe we could make a community out of it. Maybe it's already there, waiting for us.

Very weirdly, we have it on ancient authority that the intellectual burden of pursuing these questions is a much less onerous task than the psychic burden we take on ourselves the more we try to avoid the questions. We have Socrates, of course, who tells us that the unexamined life is hardly worth the effort, but it's Jesus of Nazareth I'm thinking of. He insists that his instruction, in spite of all the ways it overturns the social conventions of his day and our own, is actually an easier yoke and a lighter burden than what we're accustomed to taking on in our feverish avoidance of what real neighborliness, in word and deed, requires. There is so much to overcome in the work of seeing rightly, but a good joke, when we receive it *feelingly*, can jump our defenses in an instant. Consider Will Ferrell's poor, exhausted anchor looking hard at the static deep within and finding nothing save Black people he wants cleared out and poor people coming at him with swords. The sham is tiring. Peer pressure is forever. Figuring out what you have to do and say and believe—or pretend to believe—to get by can wear a body out. Playing along with the farce will leave you fatigued.

"Come out from among it!" one can almost hear a comedy, an accurate song, a good teacher, a Greek chorus, or a thing of beauty say. Step away from the sham. Act natural. Act natural? If only it were so simple. Every day is a do-over distinguishing light from darkness, because at the heart of any sham is a desire to be social, an easily malformed one but a desire nonetheless, a desire to be *a part of* something instead of feeling alone and *apart from* everything and everyone. It can go very badly, even taking a turn for the murderous, but it's a sacred longing not to be despised. A moment's consideration will afford us any number of examples of the ways our heart's desire to be social—to count, to be heard, to somehow matter—is enlisted, exploited, preyed upon, and harnessed repeatedly to maximize financial profits. But honoring it with honesty, mercy, candor, and kindness might be the soul of seriousness itself.

Step away from the sham.

"I wanna go someplace where we know somebody who can plug us into the social pipeline." As far as I can tell, there's isn't a person alive who isn't somehow spoken for in these words from *Dumb and Dumber*, offered with desperate longing to Harry Dunne (Jeff Daniels) by Lloyd

Christmas (Jim Carrey), a man for whom a murdered parakeet has come to serve as a final straw, a sacred sign indicating that it's high time the two men finally set out to make something of themselves. Even if we somehow wave it away out of disgust or despair to get a little distance from it, "the social pipeline" remains maddeningly in view for everyone, still staring us down in one way or another. Not a bad name for the state of play, but how will this work? Are dignity and self-possession still a thing? How do we avoid entering yet again or, as we often find ourselves doing, unwittingly perpetuating one more sham? Is the pursuit of true religion—right thought and right action—even possible?

I like to think of thinking—*really* thinking—as a party to which everyone is invited. It's a party where we have much to talk about and share, but it also involves being alive to the dangers of not really listening, to the living death *not* listening is, as we know we have to hold our favorite ideas about ourselves and others lightly. We often have to let go to really see, to give way, to allow for the unexpected wisdom of others, to see that we're not seeing. There's a way of envisioning people, a way of talking about ourselves, that invites us to really *take care*, an intensely attentive hospitality so wary of the dangers of distorted thinking that it won't allow the social pipeline, for instance, to be perceived or portrayed as some kind of zero-sum game.

HUMAN LEARNING IS NOT OWNED

Way back in the twentieth century, I witnessed an exchange that stayed with me as a kind of standard for what I'm talking about. I was in my third year of teaching high-school English, staring blankly at a copier in the "Teacher's Work Room," when a student walked in to retrieve something or other for someone in authority.

"Hey," a colleague shouted in a mock-bully tone. "What are you doing in here? How *dare* you impersonate a teacher!"

The student rolled her eyes and moved along, but a nearby faculty member seized the moment to say something subversively helpful: "Isn't that what we're all doing?"

What a saving rhetorical question, this casual assertion that all the world is something of a stage with each of us sometimes poorly, sometimes persuasively, putting on our sincere acts of make-believe and hoping for the best. I'm always heartened by a bemused word of self-deprecation from someone in the thick of things, a wink that acknowledges the sense in which we're all shamming our way through life. But the moment probably lingered longer because of the wide-eyed response I received when I recounted the exchange to a friend who taught at another high school: "No one would *ever* say that at my school."

What an unfortunate environment to imagine. No adult allowed to wonder aloud if you're a pretender? No honest expression of confusion permitted? No voicing the very-worth-asking question of whether education is genuinely occurring in the hours we share with students? No openness to the possibility that perhaps, every so often, the service we were supposedly rendering wasn't even remotely carrying over, that we weren't *actually* teaching?

So much can get lost in the theatrics of expertise, of trying to make an impression, of trying to demand—as if it were possible—respect. And that quieter work of living out a vocation—knowing and enjoying what we're good at and experiencing the thrill of doing it well—can get buried in that all-too-religious commitment to keep up appearances. The subtler question of how to be alive to the living presence of others often goes unasked.

My memory of that incident returned to me recently when I overheard an English professor friend, Annette Sisson, casually posit a revolutionary saying that begins to thaw something within me whenever I recall it: "Human learning is not owned." Ah yes, how could I have forgotten such a fact when I feel it in my bones? Learning is a communal movement, and it won't easily abide a restlessly egotistical acquisitiveness or a nervous clawing after competitive advantage. Of course, in the ongoing effort to be a good steward of my own realizations, I might do well to try to own or *own up to* them, but it's never as if I have only my own isolated self to thank for whatever I manage to realize. Like any form of meaning, learning largely happens by way of the mental labor of others, whether dead or alive, passed down, gingerly handed over, and sometimes *possibly* facilitated by one person sharing their attention collection with another. People come to consciousness in relationship. This is the phenomenon—how it enlivens a heart!—of shared meaning. It takes two to mean, after all. And no one has their meaning alone.

RELIGION IS NOT A FIXED SCRIPT

All learning is shared learning. All insight is *communally* transmitted. All eloquence is borrowed. There is likely no wisdom you've gleaned for which you don't have someone else to thank. Your understanding of your own world has come to you—and will keep coming to you— by the hands of others. It's been *traditioned* unto you. If we'd like to, we're welcome to describe an awareness of this state of affairs as a *religious* awareness, but I'm not sure what the application of the adjective adds to plain old awareness. Religion, like stories, promises, and rituals, is just one more social fact. It happens to us. The *what* of what happened is the actual content of *what* got traditioned, the marching orders we've found ourselves following. It's what's been ingrained in our thinking.

Do you like what's been ingrained in your thinking?

Would you like to see it turned around, transformed, or revolutionized?

Do you feel stuck?

It's a beautiful and wondrous thing to recall that a person's religion need not be a fixed script. While it may be the case that, beginning at birth, we learn by way of pattern recognitions, mimicking what's being modeled for us, looking to have our patterns and models confirmed and reconfirmed, we're also often made to discover that many paradigms to which we're prone to clutch are, in fact, faulty, and our thinking undergoes a holy shift. Salvation comes to our household. It's not even an especially rare happening.

As wandering pilgrims always in search of a more coherent story, we can change, convert, reform, and stumble into new habits of being at any given moment. People can wake up to themselves at any time. We aren't irredeemably stuck. Or as the novelist Ralph Ellison once remarked, we may very well be *stuck* with our relatives, but we get to *choose* our ancestors.[2] There's no denying the fact of our particular lineage, however embarrassing and dysfunctional it might be, but we can step into or draw from a different, more life-giving trajectory whenever we please.

What Ellison is referring to specifically is his refusal, especially as a young Black artist, to allow anyone to constrain his range of influences, the hodgepodge that would make up his inner creative core, his source material, his attention collection. According to popular dictates, he was expected to have certain influences like Langston Hughes and Richard Wright, but he insisted on adopting and holding close to his heart particular ancestors like William Faulkner, Ernest Hemingway, and T. S. Eliot in constant defiance of what had been placed before him as appropriate categories and genres. He felt himself free to draw inspiration from anyone he liked: "I learned very early that in the realm of the imagination all people and their ambitions and their interests could meet."[3] In this sense, we're perfectly free to write our own ticket at any time, to choose our own traditions as we discern which voices, tales, and creative offerings might serve us well in becoming what we long to be, to receive the witness of others, whether near or far, by making *their* witness a part of our own. As individuals, we each have an alarmingly profound degree of personal power in preparing within ourselves certain inner resources from which we can constantly draw, certain dreams in our hearts that won't leave us alone. We'll want to choose our ancestors carefully because we don't have to wait for the teleprompter to break to discover what's in there, what reserves we have or don't have in the work of keeping it together, imagining our neighbors righteously and, generally speaking, playing well with others. We can follow up or track down any question or insight we'd like at any time with honesty and energy, and we're right to do so because our inner life is always underway. And so much will depend on the channels to which we choose to remain tuned in.

It could almost seem appropriate to ask each other from time to time, "How's your religion coming along? How's *it* going? . . . Is there a fever in your mind that won't go away? Mind if I prescribe a poem?"

You never hear people put it this way, and I don't intend to start a trend, but when we consider the ever-evolving process of a person's thinking, the way a person imagines and organizes the world, it could almost seem appropriate to ask each other from time to time, "How's your religion coming along? How's *it* going? Born again or the same old same old? Did you successfully distinguish darkness from light in the course of your day? Is there a fever in your mind that won't go away? Mind if I prescribe a poem?"

If certain organizing fictions or controlling stories are inevitable vehicles of human culture (and culture—like religion—is an insanely large abstraction big enough to include the big ideas behind the big behavior, the big buildings, and the big blowups that we're trying to somehow account for with words), a self-conscious grappling over what actually animates us might be the most essential, sacred task any of us can take on. No human development—what a phrase—without it. What am I up to and why? Who are my ancestors, and why am I choosing them?

WE ARE WHAT WE PRETEND TO BE

Another way of putting these questions—and if it helps, we can feel free to call it THE QUESTION OF OUR LIVES—is this: What are the movements, *the ancestral lines*, within and along which we'd like, or hope, to find our own lives in deep continuity? It might be important to add, for emphasis, *because they already are.* It's already the case that our values—the ones we have and probably not the ones we expend vast amounts of energy trying to appear to have—are visible via the value judgments we make all day every day. It might involve a little digging, but a thumbnail sketch is already possible. You'll know us by our fruit, as that peasant artisan prophet again reminds us. Certain themes are, no doubt, already apparent. Like it or not, the claim, the call, the continuities along which my own lived existence sits can probably be reasonably guessed at even now. I often hope, for instance, that someone might be able to say of me that my seeking of God's reign and righteousness wasn't entirely theoretical, that my story somehow also told, from time to time, the old, old story of Jesus and his love.

Of course, this road is fraught with many a paradox. Pick an ancient or contemporary source of wisdom, and you'll be told to avoid self-consciousness, to not let the right hand know what the left hand is doing, to lose your life in order to find it, and to do good in secret lest you find yourself doing it *to be seen* doing it. "We are what we pretend to be," instructs Kurt Vonnegut, "so we must be careful about what we pretend to be."[4] Can this provocatively Oscar Wildean adage be taken up helpfully?

I think so. We take it up whenever we follow up on our own loves well, *knowingly* drawing inspiration from people and ideas we find beautiful and imitating them like wide-eyed children do. If comparison is the thief of joy, then perhaps curiosity *without* undue comparison *plus* wonder can equal inspiration.[5] We know inspiration when we're exposed to what feels like a saving bit of information, when we see, hear, or experience another person and find ourselves longing to know what they seem to know so wisely and well. This, too, is the social pipeline. How do we level with ourselves with good humor and humility concerning our own longing for meaning? We can begin by letting ourselves wonder why it is that *this* and not *that* seems to resonate. A commitment to becoming aware of what's going on in your mind requires confession, but it's also a matter of taking careful stock of what's within your bag of treasured things, your attention collection. There's no getting away from the equation that is the ineluctable relation between your output and your input.

I think, too, of the Catholic anarchist activist Dorothy Day, whose commitment to the love of God took the form of holding all things in common with the disenfranchised poor in houses of hospitality still at large in the Catholic Worker movement. She often passed time in prison, whether for protesting American war making or demanding a woman's right to vote. She refused the rush on the part of onlookers to decree her a saint because she sensed that behind the compliment there lurked the suggestion that only some people are called to the alleged extremes of Christian practice: "Don't call me a saint; I don't want to be dismissed so easily." How would she like to be remembered, then? As someone who read the novels of Dostoevsky well.

This formulation of aspiration gets at the question of ancestral lines. We get to reach out to those voices that have reached out to us, and by doing so, we extend their reach even further. One could observe, for instance, that Dostoevsky's life was, from at least a few angles, an unmitigated disaster of addiction, betrayal, and no small amount of anti-Semitism. But if Day's witness to his witness is to be believed, his own creative faithfulness to his novelistic visions of a broken and beautiful world can't be separated from the Catholic Worker movement, easily one of the most persuasive prophetic movements of our time. His feats of attentiveness attended to hers in the very way that, if we want them to, hers will attend to ours. In the realm of the prophetic imagination, everybody's profoundest, most lyrical longings for the world can be made to meet up with everybody else's. There remain so many ways to say—to testify concerning—who and what rings true.

TASTE AND SEE

Once you begin to see it this way, these shout-outs are visible everywhere. It's the ongoing paying of tribute, the acknowledgment of sources, that leads to many an homage that can't help but articulate yet another mental breakthrough, another instance in which one person's creative effort somehow releases the creative capacities of another's. In R.E.M.'s "E-Bow the Letter," Michael Stipe extends the high five of gratitude to Patti Smith, for whom it's often as if her every song, story, or poem is a clear-eyed, ecstatic expression of thanksgiving to someone else. Bob Dylan's "Last Thoughts on Woody Guthrie" doesn't name Guthrie until the very end of a very long poem, but by the end, the sanity-saving service Guthrie rendered to Dylan is abundantly evident. Human beings everywhere and in every time make it past or through or to the end of their long loneliness by believing other human beings who pass their own inspirations down through a long chronicling of cosmic plainspeak, of trying to say what they see. One true believer after another. Or as Dylan once put it on the subject of his life's work, "I believe the songs."[6]

Needless to say, I don't think of this as an evasion of creed, community, or doctrine. I would hope that we are all collectors and believers of good stories, songs, and all manner of artfulness. It is in so many ways the good work to be done. We get to stand by our jams with our very lives, living up to them somehow as gifts of discernment. We don't receive them at all till we do. How else would a body go about tasting and seeing that life or even the Creator of life is good? We can stare at reality for a lifetime without seeing it, but we learn to see it better, more righteously, when we choose our ancestors well, when we pick up and examine what they placed in the path for our everlasting benefit.

And they—our ancestors—really did collect and set all kinds of things down to pass along for our approval, saving them and treasuring them, one feat of attentiveness at a time, for the joy of someone else treasuring what they found sacred. The hope of civilization resides in the attention collections of the many unknowns to whose powers of canonization we owe so much. So much goodness has been carried over. We get to pass it on too. The poet Mary Rose O'Reilley describes the process aptly: "People all over the world are doing very hard things—turning the other cheek, giving all they have to the poor, eating potatoes without salt—because some confused and yawning student took a note."[7] We live off the generosity of those who pay heed. What feats of curiosity and acts of attentiveness do we owe ourselves and others in the here and now and later?

THE WAY OF THE GIFT

There is so much that distracts us from hearing this question and from even accessing a sense of how to begin, but the urge to make righteous meaning persists. One of the chief obstacles to treasuring the insights available to us in the relentlessly communal work of waking up to ourselves and others is also a primary target of this book: the defensive mechanism of disassociation when it comes to what we think we have in hand when we say *religion*. Rightly understood, it's a cue for renewed curiosity concerning what we're doing with ourselves, for what others seem to be about at their core, and a cause for wonder. Why cling to the myth of critical attachment as if it were a life preserver against the complications of other people? Is there a lasting refuge in disassociation?

Believing there might be is understandable given the mess of things we've inherited under the moniker of religion. Understandable to a point, I should say. And I'm helped here by the wisdom of the character John Ames, a seventy-six-year-old Iowan pastor in Marilynne Robinson's novel *Gilead*, which is a long diary written by Ames to a son whose young adulthood he knows he won't live to see. He worries that his son might fall into the disassociating rush, as many have done and will do in view of the lived fact of spiritual abuse. Ames, as the latest and likely last of a long line of pastors, offers no defense of the church's failings, but he seizes the occasion to express a broader vision for the way he hopes his son might come to understand the church's witness and the disillusionment that often accompanies it.

He begins by noting that as a child, he himself was possessed by a naive but telling misimpression of the metal steeples of churches. He presumed that churches everywhere nobly affixed crosses at great heights to absorb the lightning that might otherwise endanger smaller structures in their communities, purposefully seeking to take the hit in a gesture of communal gallantry. He came to know better and to understand that not all churches were situated on the Great Plains, that not all pastors were like his father, and that many a church organization has fallen woefully short of what could be meaningfully referred to as demonstrably moral community. He wants his son to understand that he's exceedingly aware of this last fact. He knows that there is so much anyone with a conscience must decry in that which passes for church and that his own experience of the church has been limited and unique "in many senses" and perhaps "in every sense." In view of this, he concedes that the hope of lived righteousness in church might be done for apart from a weighty *unless*:

> Unless it really is a universal and transcendent life, unless the bread is the bread and the cup is the cup everywhere, in all circumstances, and it is a time with the Lord in Gethsemane that comes for everyone, as I deeply believe. . . . It all means more than I can tell you. So you must not judge what I know by what I find words for. If I could only give you what my father gave me. No, what the Lord has given me and must also give you. But I hope you will put yourself in the way of the gift.[8]

Say what you must about your inheritance. Perhaps you'll feel called upon to betray it in more ways than one. But put yourself—*keep* yourself—in the way of the gift at all cost. Understand the joy and the obligation to carry what goodness there is in it forward. This admonition is at the heart of the sensibility I hope to urge upon others in regard to our talk of religion. It's a disposition that allows for disaffection but also disallows the prejudgment that amounts to preemptive casting out of others, those ignorant souls whose beliefs we're all too prone to believe have somehow already reached the shallow bottom. Ames hopes his son will know to place himself in the way—the path—of the gift in all things, including the possibility that his own father was a steward of a sacred mystery for which words will often—must even necessarily—fail. Because it's in the nature of a gift, the offering and the reception, to create relationship and to overcome that which divides, one can't remain in the way of the gift and also definitively disassociate. When a gift occurs, we see ourselves in others, our very lives sustained by the grace of others, and we find we can hardly hold ourselves apart. The gift occasions communion, that wholeness for which we're all longing in one way or another most of the time.

What are we to do with our craving for order and meaning? Stay in the way of the gift. Consider all that might yet come to you—all that might yet remain in circulation *by way of* you—as a living tradition. Stay within the line of its movement. Make something of the Earthseed you discern. Make it available. We know well the burden of being a member (letting yourself be *re*membered) within a community, but there are also times we might, at any moment, begin—or begin again—to experience this burden as a gift.

And this again places us firmly within a particular paradox because without the burden of belonging in some way to other people, we have no way of experiencing ourselves *as* a gift to others. At such times, our deep desire to be telling and following a story, to be of help and to share our enthusiasms with somebody—anybody—is without anything we can see as a genuine outlet. Without the flow of the gift, we have no access to the social pipeline, no means of making sense of ourselves. What are we to do with the mad turbulence of our own self-consciousness? Consider the gift.

What are we to do with our craving for order and meaning? Stay in the way of the gift.

INTERNATIONAL WATERS WITH IMAGINARY LINES ON THEIR SURFACE

"It's hard to overstate how deep the need can get for things to make sense," observes the reclusive fortysomething narrator, Sean Phillips, in John Darnielle's *Wolf in White Van*.[9] And in my thinking and hoping concerning the way of the gift, he often arises in my mind as a kind of test case, a frontier of longing, sadness, and good humor. A recent addition to my attention collection, I think of him as a dark marvel and a gift to my understanding of myself and to others of my generation.

The story of the gunshot wound that left his face grotesquely disfigured at seventeen is only completely spelled out on the final page of the novel, but even as we're deprived till then of certain details, we're made to see that his will to matter and his will to mean can't be isolated from this event. As a teenager with a love for *Conan the Barbarian* paperbacks, late-night televangelist programs, Dungeons and Dragons, and the coin-operated video game Xevious ("Playing it was like watching flowers bloom"[10]), his chosen ancestors are, at first blush, unconventional and, by popular estimate, unworthy. But Phillips bestows upon each such depth and lyricism that his passionate pilgrimage leaves his parents and most of his peers in a pale of lukewarm denial. He is alive—eye-rubbingly alive—to the minute particulars around him and the beauty, the goodwill, and the subtle but devastating hypocrisies he's expected to take on as his own in what passes for the real world. As early as sixth grade and into his earning of a modest income officiating a mail-order role-playing game called Trace Italian, Phillips is a purveyor and seeker of "true vision,"[11] and his tragic situation renders him an extraordinarily keen observer of the human drama even as it mostly excludes him. It's as if he takes people individually and every pop-culture artifact placed before him more seriously than they take themselves. Though pulled into despair by the delusions and denials normalized within his family, he pushes through with a tender and affectionate determination to see them rightly: "I try to be careful about the things I think."[12] It takes courage to see sometimes.

He finds his attention held by the memory of a child's voice on the beach in a commercial for a game called Stay Alive ("I'm the sole

survivor!") and the way certain words seem to address him personally ("Anything that involved the word *star* always sounded like it was
speaking directly to me"[13]). His chronicling of passions and remembered interactions makes the novel a kind of puzzle that compels us
to ruminate almost desperately over how he arrived where he is, a puzzle that remains largely intact even after that last page. But there's an
exchange with his father I find extraordinarily evocative, profoundly
heartbreaking, and somehow triumphantly familiar. It's a memory
from his teenage years in—you guessed it—the '80s.

Sean Phillips's father yells at the television. The yelling involves a
requisite turning up of the volume, and this makes the family dinner-
time a kind of hours-long roar of noise. In this instance, it's Muammar
Gaddafi at whom Sean's father rages, and he tries to pull Sean in, to no
avail: "I couldn't make myself care much about it: it seemed like nothing; I couldn't keep any of it straight." Amid stories of gas prices, bites
of meatloaf, and Phillips telling his mother he likes the sauce, an overheard phrase gets him thinking: "American ships in Libyan water." At
a commercial break, he tries to jump in.

"Dad, are Libyan waters different from other waters?"

His mother tries to discourage the conversation before it can begin,
but his father responds, "They're differ-
ent because of sovereignty."

"But there aren't any actual lines on
the water or anything."

"They have maps and coordinates."

"Right, but the water—"

"The water is the same."

**There is no dropping
of the microphone
because this is
where it ends.**

There is no dropping of the microphone because this is where it
ends. But in the narrative now, Phillips tells us how pleased he was to
let the matter rest there "out in international waters with imaginary
lines on their surface that no one could actually see."[14]

Take that, you mad, mad world. And may we all find in the gift a way in which to put such extraordinary moments of seeing, this alienated instance of true vision, this steadfast refusal of one tired old teleprompter. Perhaps the novel is one way. And there's also the way that overcomes estrangement whenever we put a truly open-ended question to someone else and truly wait quietly and expectantly for a response. When we manage that one—and there are friendly folks the world over who are managing it even now—we can know that the way of the gift is being embodied somewhere. It happens whenever we pay proper heed to one another in the giving and receiving of witness, whenever people *actually communicate* with one another. When that near-miraculous-feeling transaction occurs, perhaps it's appropriate to consider it an exemplary instance of true religion, the process whereby people experience themselves and their resources—their ancestors too—as gifts.

When we think of it this way, religion is perhaps most helpfully conceived of as the question of what tales and traditions—collections—our lives embody. Everybody embodies *something*. We're never not embodying. If religion is a concept we might begin to apply to ourselves with the same ease we project it upon others, it might even expand the horizon of personal honesty and help keep before ourselves the hope of being—or proving to have been—at least every so often true. Perhaps there are unexpected resources available to us in this lifelong work.

4

I LEARNED IT BY WATCHING YOU

Science fiction properly conceived, like all serious fiction, however funny, is a way of trying to describe what is in fact going on, what people actually do and feel, how people relate to everything else in this vast stack, this belly of the universe, this womb of things to be and tomb of things that were, this unending story.

—Ursula K. Le Guin

At the age of five, I was home sick one day when my mother placed before me an unexpected resource. It was issue number 189 of *The Incredible Hulk.* The cover featured the green goliath standing at the mouth of a cave holding an unconscious woman in his arms as tears streamed down his face. Something's gone horribly awry. I couldn't read at the time, but my mother read Hulk's words, which set the scene, aloud: "Somebody hurt Hulk's friend . . . and when Hulk finds them . . . Hulk will smash!"

Hulk had me at "smash!" There was an energy in the image that won me over from that moment on. This is my first memory of a comic book, a portal of color and strange goings-on. A gift of vision, a means to holding out my own fear, worry, and wonder—my own experience even as a child—at a different angle. In time, I would stare wistfully at skylines and mountain ranges and visualize what Hulk, if provoked, would do to them. This was my entry point to art and creative receptivity. I imagine that for my mother, it was something of a random catechesis in the sense that she likely spied the image on a metal rack at a drugstore or gas station and figured Hulk might draw me away from the television for a while. But I was marked for life. Even now, I devote a fair amount of time to contemplating the challenges, opportunities, and quandaries confronting Doctor Bruce Banner.

As you must know, Bruce Banner has a Hulk problem. Pelted by gamma rays while conducting a desert experiment involving the detonation of an atomic bomb, too much anger transforms him into a creature of escalating and almost limitless physical strength. His mood swings can bring down buildings. For a five-year-old, that can sound rather awesome, but Hulk first appeared before me, in the image of a weeping monster, as something of a tragic figure. The more I studied his—or their—existence, the more the Hulk situation seemed to apply to real-life subjects. Despite his considerable intellectual gifts, Banner's Hulk problem means he has a hard time finding a context in which he can be his best, safest, and most meaningfully sociable self. I could relate. I still can.

Power is relative to context. Bruce Banner understands this as well as anyone in the earth's long chronicle. He also knows feelingly that what we do with our anger is what we will have done with our lives. Hulk lore, like Marvel Comics lore, like science-fiction lore, has a way of getting at what we're up against, what we're up to, how it all feels. It scratches an itch. It brings to consciousness questions and possibilities that are otherwise obscured and even buried.

"In a science fiction story," Philip K. Dick once explained, "one projects what has been a personal inner experience into a milieu; it becomes socially shared, hence discussable."[1] That's right: Discussable. A difficult-to-talk-about thing is magically brought into the space of the talkaboutable. Consider the Hulk.

You can perhaps see how contemplating Bruce Banner's plight fits squarely in my course titled Religion and Science Fiction. Those two abstractions are bookends of most everything I like to talk about. Where else can we go to see the big ideas that make us miserable, jerk us around like mixed-up marionettes, decree that the way things are is the way they have to be, might be seen as consensual fictions? And if they're only time-honored fictions, we can ask, why don't we begin to withdraw our consent? What would happen then? Maybe we're at an amazing juncture full of unforeseen possibilities right now.

Money? A collective hallucination.

Progress? For whom and according to what?

Authority? That's an open question since what we call *authorized* is relative to what functions as a teleprompter in our lives, who it is we're willing to credit with magical powers of authorization, those *authors* of our fates we anxiously look to, to be told what's permissible and possible.

Boundaries? Well, they've been drawn up over time, and they somehow stuck. Whose designations do we find necessary, healthy, or even sacred? Everything depends upon our sacred designations: private property, sacraments, militarized zones, places of worship, border patrols.

Science fiction addresses these questions by way of thought experiments. Throw people into the distant future and see what happens. Or hurl them backward into an inconceivably ancient past. Introduce technology that completely flips the script of what we think we know. Bring aliens into the equation and ask them about their standards for how to rightly measure intelligent life. Who's civilized *now*?

SCIENCE FICTION BREAKS THE ICE

Like nothing else can, science fiction invites us to take the temperature of our own strange behavior, to note the outrageous arbitrariness at work in our organizing fictions, and to proceed more wonderingly in our conception of ourselves. It raises the question of how we've been imprinted. At its best, in my own life it performs nothing less than a prophetic and revivifying function. It makes me more alive to incongruities I've allowed to become normalized. And as any lover of sci-fi understands implicitly, the contradictions were normalized *for* me long before I was born. Do I care to live up to that one *Star Trek* episode that got me thinking about all the subtle ways the Borg represents the strong forces of spirit-deadening conformity? Am I a red-pill or a blue-pill person?

Taking science fiction in—reading, watching, and talking about it—is one of my favorite ways of doing battle with my own thoughtlessness. And against the caricature of the sci-fi enthusiast as a geek or a nerd who refuses to grow up, I'd like to somehow cling—for dear life—to the sense of play that comes easiest to us in childhood while also arguing that the lover of sci-fi might best be seen as someone peculiarly determined to *keep* growing up and evolving, hunting down tales, analogies, and even facts that serve to sharpen our sense of wonder at the weird worlds we're in.

To begin to wonder, as Aristotle instructs us, is to begin to philosophize, and philosophy is bad news for bad religion. As I've come to see it, science-fiction culture itself is a space in which to plot resistance to all the bad religion that shapes our thinking, asserting its pressure in our minds and nervous systems, narrowing our sense of what's possible, coloring our perceptions of people and events.

I have in mind the phenomenon of *ideology*, which often appears to be the moving target at which my favorite science fiction takes aim.

Like brainwash, ideology isn't something anyone is likely to knowingly avow. But the word is useful in naming a creeping madness we're usually powerless to detect. Ideology is what you have to believe in order to not hate yourself completely for what you've already decided to say and do. In this sense, it's mostly improvised. Ideology is the supreme nut—the hardness of head and heart, the thickness of falsehood—that generations of prophets and free thinkers have sought to crack, the mind-forged manacles William Blake warned us about, the frozen sea inside the hardened heart.

Science-fiction culture itself is a space in which to plot resistance to all the bad religion that shapes our thinking.

Science fiction breaks the ice and picks the lock on the doors of perception. Like any good parable, poem, film, or song, it functions as a call to *keep thinking* when everyone else appears to have stopped. This might name the lonely virtue we honor when we call someone a nerd. Science fiction almost tricks us into being nerds, spitting us out at the end of a story only to discover we've succumbed to an insight we never signed up for. Momentarily deprived of our powers of prejudgment and presupposition, it catches us, like a good joke, with our defenses down. Rod Serling describes the process as something he discovered while composing revelatory vignettes of our moral weirdness for *The Twilight Zone*: "I found it was all right to have Martians saying things Democrats and Republicans could never say."[2]

A SONG IS A MIND CRYING OUT

Consider the two-thousand-plus-year-old Gallifreyan, a Time Lord, who comes to us as the two-hearted protagonist of the *Doctor Who* series. In its fifty-year history, the question "Doctor *who?*" has been wisely left unanswered. As a character conveniently capable of regeneration, they've been played by fourteen different actors, at last count, each of whom crafts a unique iteration of a being who is a lives-long learner with fiercely intelligent love for the human race spanning space and time. Whatever the planet or historical period their time-traveling spacecraft the TARDIS (Time and Relative Dimensions in Space) gets them to, they size up the scene with a moral and intellectual rigor that upsets the dehumanizing status quo of the day. Ever alive to what everyone else has yet to notice, the Doctor doesn't ultimately *miss* people, and they can pull what is interesting out of anything and anyone. As our best nerd, they often seem hell-bent on persuading friends and companions to be *better* nerds, to find themselves more interesting, to live up to the complexity of their own consciousness and that of their fellow creatures, to somehow rise above their conditioning.

That call to think again and more and further, to be born again once again through the renewal of the mind, is a call the Doctor also heeds when surrounded by friends, alleged enemies, and those they might be tempted to view as lower life forms. An especially telling instance in which the actor David Tennant's Doctor gets schooled for their inattentiveness occurs in an episode called "Planet of the Ood." Having once encountered the Ood as the cheerfully docile servants of humans in the forty-second century, they presume that the Ood are what their minders conceived and acquired them as, creatures too simple-minded to desire or dream of anything more than their current lot in life: "Born to serve."

Everything changes when the Doctor and their companion, Donna Noble, a present-day Londoner leaving her temp work to see what traveling in the TARDIS might yield, hear a song that leads them to an escaped Ood bleeding to death from bullet wounds. The Doctor had experienced the Ood as servers offering various forms of assistance, but now they've heard one calling out telepathically. "That was the song," the Doctor explains. "It was his mind crying out." With the help of a map alleged to chart Ood Operations, they begin to see that distribution centers lead to processing plants and eventually make their way to a restricted warehouse in which the Ood are kept in containers. Having been initially wowed by the technological advances and the intergalactic distances traveled by her forty-second-century descendants, Donna is disgusted and appalled: "A great big empire built on slavery."

"It's not so different from your time," the Doctor observes.

"Oy!" she exclaims. "I haven't got slaves."

"Who do you think made your clothes?"

Consider the perceived necessities brought to consciousness—made more discussable—by a moment like this. There's an especially telling exchange when the Doctor and Donna try to enlist the help of Solana Mercurio, the charming and clever head of public relations for Ood Operations. Might she be persuaded to blow the whistle? If the people of Earth knew what was being done to the Ood, Donna reasons, they wouldn't stand for it.

"Oh, don't be so stupid," Solana exclaims. "Of course they know."

How can that be? Solana says, "They don't ask. Same thing."

The Doctor weighs in: "Solana, the Ood aren't born like this. They can't be. A species born to serve could never evolve in the first place. What does the company do to make them obey?"

"That's nothing to do with me."

"Oh, what, because you don't *ask?*" As ever, the Doctor never stops trying to pull us out of whatever trance we're in, whatever bits of observable reality we've kept isolated from one another as if to purposefully avoid the moral realization that could change everything for the better. Over a millennium or so, the Doctor has observed their share of ideology and all the ways we have of misnaming progress, civilization, and development. The era and the alien species might differ, but the groupthink remains the same. Even the Doctor falls into it from time to time: "Last time I met the Ood, I never thought. I never asked . . . I didn't need the map. I should have *listened*."

The Doctor here administers a self-admonition, setting a courageously moral example for me and my fellow nerds as they have for over half a century. The challenge is to respond more creatively to incoming data, to learn and act upon a literacy of wonder, that habit of attentiveness that is obviously a moral and a political literacy as well. In episode after episode, the Doctor shows us what a bearer of extraordinary consciousness looks like while also offering hints and indications for seeing how ours is extraordinary too. Like their companions, we're all one moment of concentration away from seeing some crucial something we had yet to let ourselves see. We'll have to widen our horizon of expectation if we're to wake up to the mess we're in *and* all the strange and beautiful ways we might yet turn the world around.

THE THINGS YOU MAKE UP . . . THE RULES

As if we were all fantastic beings—because every day offers opportunity to learn again that we are—the Doctor invites us to gaze upon one another. The Doctor also exemplifies the manner in which good humor, compassion, and a well-chosen word can occasionally overcome blind power. We're admonished to dwell no longer in unawareness concerning our own weird surroundings (Who built this? What holds these people in awe? What are they afraid of? What leaps of faith were taken and why?). *Doctor Who* enthusiasts ask what's been *normalized* from on high, why we've gone along with the plan, and what lovely and extraordinary things might happen if we stopped.

And what goes for the Whovian goes for anyone with a hole in the heart that can only be filled by science fiction. Generally we're already up for this kind of thing because we're desperate to flip the given script. The *received* religion—which is the *reigning* religion—won't do. Uncritical subservience is, as ever, the problem. Deferential fear be damned.

Driven by their own curiosity, lovers of science fiction are *eager* to immerse themselves in strange new worlds where their customary paradigms stop working. They feel the need to grapple their way toward better ones, to dream further and more deeply. As the Time Lord themselves (the Peter Capaldi iteration) puts it, "I believe I haven't seen everything. I don't know. It's funny, isn't it? The things you make up—*the rules*. . . . Still, that's why I keep traveling. To be proved wrong."

It is precisely here that the Doctor serves as a kind of apex nerd. This is the call to answer the ethical summons to think beyond conventions, our comfort zones, our preferred ideologies, to see what we're not seeing, the determination to be ever wary of our own peculiar habits of inattentiveness. The Doctor sees past the infrastructures of bad ideas that seize people's hearts and shape their behaviors and beckons out of friend and alleged foe alike curiosity and latent conviviality. Everything depends upon this spirit, this sacred intuition, this *ancient know-how* handed down. The good religion the Doctor sets in motion *one more time* is that story and song through which human coherence, figurative and literal, is passed down to others as tradition, as a living possibility.

Whether interacting with Rosa Parks, Charles Dickens, or a Dalek, the Doctor dramatizes the joys and demands of Beloved Community in a variety of settings, insisting that everything matters, that insignificance is never an option. This frame of mind applies to the space-time continuum a sense of indebtedness famously articulated by George Eliot: "The growing good of the world is partly dependent on unhistoric acts . . . that things are not so ill with you and me as they might have been, is half owing to the number who lived faithfully a hidden life, and rest in unvisited tombs."[3]

Earthseed and other signs of life—other forms of moral serious-ness—are handed down and made available. Such a song, should it in any sense remain the same, can serve as a vessel of unbroken solidarity. As redemption songs do, it infiltrates our thinking, lyrically signaling the fact of kindred spirits who once articulated a hoped-for rightness that might yet register one fine day. According to this familiar trope, the wisdom of ancient traditions is nothing less than the carefully cul-tivated, long-haul awareness of those who precede us, once ancient but now contemporary if anyone out there has an ear to hear and an eye to see. It turns out that those imaginative, long-suffering, long-dead, hidden faithful who saw fit to preserve, copy, and write so many things down often knew exactly what they were on about. The present doesn't often recognize them. And the future reveals them. Can they get a witness in the here and now?

AN ETHIC IS A WAY OF THINKING

To really receive a witness—to bear, embody, give, and pass it on—is not a matter of making a purchase, acquiring information, or absent-mindedly downloading a song. Witness calls for *withness*, getting in on someone else's act, a live grappling giving way to a realization that *this* has to do with *that*. A realization can't be force-fed on a person or a people, but it can be taken up and lived up to. Not a possession but an experience. To receive the witness of another is to enter into a vision inaccessible to us in isolation. We realize ourselves as members of one another, compelled to act accordingly, finding that we can't easily *live with ourselves* if we don't.

> **To receive the witness of another is to enter into a vision inaccessible to us in isolation.**

One of the best illustrations I know of when it comes to com-municating a sacred call to revere ourselves and others comes from

Theodore Sturgeon's classically weird and wonderful 1953 sci-fi novel *More Than Human.* As Sturgeon's story goes, the next stage in human evolution doesn't come as one gifted individual arising among *Homo sapiens* but as a small group of uniquely gifted individuals who are deficient to the point of incapacity apart from access to the gifts of one another. One's a telepath; another can practice telekinesis; a couple have powers of teleportation; and one, referred to as Baby, has boundless mental capacities only communicated and experienced by way of the other four. Taken together, they form *Homo Gestalt.* They function together through a process called—wait for it—*bleshing.* And when they blesh, there's almost nothing they can't do.

Questions of how to relate, how to behave, and what might be essential to continued evolution are at the heart of the novel, which amounts to an illuminating meditation on how to know how to live. "Morals are an obedience to rules that people laid down to help you live among them,"[4] Sturgeon writes. Or as one member of *Homo Gestalt* puts it to another, "An ethic isn't a fact you can look up. It's a way of thinking."[5]

Like the rest of us (and this is why I turn to Sturgeon repeatedly), they'll have to learn to ease up, to hold things dear, and to resist proceeding through our world in a clenched-fist fashion; it's a life's work or the work of many lives over time. Joy won't be accessed through haste, fear, or anger. *More Than Human* offers us an evocative, enigmatic trail of crumbs toward *right* apprehension, one more bright electric avenue to new and better ways of conceiving ourselves and others. We don't just get to; we *have* to.

TO BE WHOLE IS TO BE PART

If you want to make it back home, you have to keep moving forward, consenting—again and again—to being transformed, to learning, revising and resisting once more the bad habit of mistaking your sense of reality for reality itself. You have to let the sweet old world, the faces of others and their words, the minute particulars of your own existence mean more than they did the day before. You have to see it all again, to respect and reconsider, thinking repentantly by thinking again, because revolution begins with a thinking mind and an open heart.

In the words of a woman named Laia Asieo Odo, a character created by Ursula K. Le Guin, who describes her as "one of the ones who walked away from Omelas,"[6] "To be whole is to be part; true journey is return."[7] Her way of putting things draws from a persistently righteous vision of social cohesion and, almost synonymously for Odo, human pleasure: "It is useless work that darkens the heart. The delight of the nursing mother, of the scholar, of the successful hunter, of the good cook, of the skilful maker, of anyone doing needed work and doing it well—this durable joy is perhaps the deepest source of human affection, and of sociality as a whole." This anthropological premise—perhaps you can feel it coming—gives rise to an entire Odonian philosophy of life well lived. Those who are formed when young, unversed in the pressures of profiteering and the maddening misperception that is private property, "will grow up with the will to do what needs doing and the capacity for joy in doing it."[8]

The witness of Odo hits its stride, in Le Guin's fiction, a few generations after her death, in Le Guin's novel *The Dispossessed*, which follows the life of a physicist named Shevek striving to live up to the Odonian vision within. The novel chronicles Shevek's own voyage of discovery concerning what constitutes true movement and the development of his own ever-burgeoning literacy of wonder.

The young Shevek we meet early in the novel finds durable joy elusive, and his mood is relentlessly darkened by labor that strikes him as completely useless. Exhausted and covered in dust like everyone else, he grows exasperated one evening when a female coworker, Gimar, sings for the thousandth time a lyric about an enigmatic "she" who somehow brings forth "green leaf from the stone" and from the rock's heart "clear water running."

"Who does?" Shevek demands. "Who's 'she'?"

"It's a miners song."

"Well, then, who's 'she'?"

"I don't know," Gimar observes, befuddled. "It's just what the song says. Isn't it what we're doing here? Bringing green leaves out of stones!"

"Sounds like religion."

"You and your fancy book-words. It's just a song."[9]

In exchanges like these, Shevek is challenged to stop mistaking his preferred abstractions for reality and to see, hear, and feel what's really in front of him. It's a life's work for all of us. In the place where Shevek is apt to congratulate himself for having successfully sniffed out "religion" (slow clap), Gimar hears instead—and sings—a poetry yet to take form, that indeed *has* taken form in the very work they're up to. She hears nothing less than a sweet record of struggle—and the taking of courage *despite* the struggle—resonating wonderfully with their own.

To call it mere fantasy or fairy tale, or, in the tired old pejorative sense, religion is a diminishment of possibility. It's also to restrict unnecessarily our realization of the organic fact of other people and the accompanying sense of solidarity none of us can live without. Every song, we get to understand, is potentially a song of myself, a song of yourself and of many other selves. What was real and of value to our ancestors might make it down to us. In a meaningful measure, we're afforded a renewed sense of orientation, a way in the wilderness where once, in our reluctance to credit much of anything or anyone, it appeared there was no way out or through.

Gimar will urge upon Shevek that more excellent way of the open hand. He will learn the life-giving trick of loving the world without looking down on it, of revering life in all of its manifestations. Like others before him, he'll take up the wonderful habit of seeing the sacred drama at work in the faces of those who cross his path and an apocalypse in the everyday.

To see an image evoked by something else is to have received a sign, and it happens all the time. The least we can do is observe consciously what's been given to us to know. We will inevitably miss so much, but we don't have to miss it all. We can be among those who insist on being awake to their own experience. It is fitting and helpful to refer to these social collectives as sacred traditions available and hospitable to us even in our fevered now. Access to poetic intuition, a revelatory understanding of the situations vouchsafed unto us, might be within reach, one lyric, novel, scripture, song, or dance away.

DISINFORMATION IS NOISE POSING AS SIGNAL

We need not look terribly far to see, *to feelingly perceive*, that it takes a village to perceive a reality. In this, too, science fiction goes ever before us. And the advance scout I look to as an apostle of misapprehension sometimes referred to as the Shakespeare of science fiction is Philip Kindred Dick.

"Reality is that which, when you stop believing in it, doesn't go away," Dick famously observed.[10] And for all the black humor one might sense in an adage like that one, it's the kind of reminder Dick was committed to placing before himself. In his sensitive, funny, and often heartbreaking view of the world, we all keep faith with one flawed but sincere vision of things or another, often looking for meaning in all the wrong places. Whether badly or beautifully, all of Dick's characters are engaged in the modest and universal struggle of try-ing to make sense, of trying to *be significant* to somebody somewhere somehow.

Disinformation (all proselytization, all the time) is the noise that drives out true significance. Worse, it is noise *posing as* significance. Or in Dick's phrase, "It is noise posing as signal so you do not even recognize it as noise." He describes the moral injury the people in the corridors of alleged power *themselves* sustain, "If you can float enough disinformation into circulation you will totally abolish everyone's contact with reality, probably your own included."[11]

Every Dick novel offers countless scenarios so overwhelmingly prescient (appliances turned companions, commercials physically accompanying you through your days and nights, corporate seizure of natural resources, people lost in their hopeless little screens) that you can find yourself checking and double-checking the publishing dates of his books. In 1965, for instance, he gave us *The Three Stigmata of Palmer Eldritch*, which features an Earth so cooked that a person can't go outside in the daytime without a body-cooling apparatus (Ant-arctica excepted, at least for now). But having sold the atmosphere to the highest bidders over time, the governments of the nations of Earth have come together to colonize what habitable planets they can find to ensure that their citizens remain profitably in motion on the treadmills of that one world religion too ubiquitous to even question: global consumerism. Enter Perky Pat Layouts.

SHARED FAITH AND BAD THINKING

The situation with Perky Pat Layouts is almost too strange to con-ceive until you come to see it as a kind of proto-online network. It's as if Dick had a vision of the internet but could only cobble an idea together with the materials at hand. Perky Pat Layouts (P. P. Layouts, Inc., based in New York City) are a hot commodity among the sad, displaced citizens-turned-colonists for whom our world is now a distant memory. With the aid of a drug called Can-D, they're left to gather in windswept hovels on arid, mostly inhospitable planets to stare at their P. P. Layouts—and they really are *layouts*, mere props involving dolls, cars, houses, electric garage doors, and all manner of miniature artifacts of a culture no longer available to them—imagining and hallucinating together in a desperate frenzy of pseudo-intimacy. It's a dystopian take akin to an age in which humans will abide anything so long as they have free Wi-Fi.

Seeking transit, they call it. And who among us doesn't hope to do just that? Dick submits for approval a meditation on the variations of *shared faith* that make for our every shot at social cohesion or, to put it old-school, communion. Every P. P. Layouts customer enters in responding to the promise of momentary transcendence, but the levels of expectation differ as well as the theories and testimonies concerning what precisely they are experiencing. On one hopeful soul named Sam Regan, Dick writes: "He himself was a believer; he affirmed the miracle of translation—the near-sacred moment in which the miniature artifacts of the layout no longer merely represented Earth but *became* Earth. And he and the others, joined together in the fusion of doll-inhabitation by means of the Can-D, were transported outside of time and local space. Many of the colonists were as yet unbelievers; to them the layouts were merely symbols of a world which none of them could any longer experience. But one by one, the unbelievers came around."

Regan finds that the hope for that little bit of human-like touch haunts him like a muscle memory every moment of every day. "Even now . . . he yearned to go back down below, chew a slice of Can-D from his hoard, and join with his fellows in the most solemn moment of which they were capable."[12]

While we find ourselves rooting for those few colonists who manage to resist the allure of Perky Pat and Can-D, those rare birds who are committed to somehow living inside their own bodies and, in spite of their lost world, trying to cultivate, plant, and harvest alien lands, Dick won't let us feel complete contempt for those who lose their way because he never lets us forget that we *are* these sad, beautiful, well-meaning people. His refusal to resort to parody or condescension renders his analysis of all the wearying behaviors humans get used to—that we settle for and even come to revel in—all the more incisive.

This question of what gets normalized, the mad, bad ideas that keep us crazy, destructive, and horribly unaware of ourselves in cycles of soul-deadening conformity, is the very question science fiction keeps in constant play. Science fiction is where we get to hold a colloquy with our own bad thinking, staging a feud with the status quo, puncturing the perverse visions that pass for normal one strange tale at a time. In an era when our bad faith actors drive us to distraction and weaponize our despair, we desperately need strange tales that bear witness to our even stranger times. We need language to describe the problem properly.

SECRETLY VIRTUOUS INSIDES

William Gibson, who gave us the novel *Neuromancer* and coined the term *cyberspace* in the '80s as he watched children stare longingly at the screens of coin-operated video games, offers a funny but amazingly astute observation concerning the service science fiction performs. For Gibson, science fiction functions as the "oven mitts" to hold and handle the red "hot casserole" of what we're all going through.[13] When so much of our experience eludes language and therefore apprehension, we need images and analogies that name and illustrate what's happening. Consider the way an episode of *Black Mirror* can appear before us like a jigsaw falling into place, synthesizing our experience, giving us a place to put it.

Gibson's novel *The Peripheral* places its near-present day protagonists into communication with the global oligarch culture of the not-all-that-distant future. Following a multipronged, semi-extinction event, referred to as the *jackpot*, only the oligarchs survived. They're referred to as the *klept* (short for *kleptocracy*). There's a form of technology that makes this communication possible, but it doesn't take much imagination to see, given the long-term destruction of the humanly inhabitable world being undertaken for the financial profit of the post-national few even now, that the klept are already among us, undertaking the free-range nihilism sometimes referred to as free enterprise.

As the novel's protagonist, Flynne, contemplates how to approach and collaborate with the klept in the future, we're given a meditation on how to take their measure in the here and now:

> People who couldn't imagine themselves capable of evil were at a major disadvantage in dealing with people who didn't need to imagine, because they already were . . . It was always a mistake, to believe those people were different, special, infected with something that was inhuman, subhuman, fundamentally other. . . . [This] reminded her . . . [that] evil wasn't glamorous, but just the result of ordinary half-assed badness, high school badness, given enough room however that might happen, to become its bigger self. Bigger, with more horrible results, but never more than the cumulative weight of ordinary human baseness.[14]

If evil is active flight from a lived realization of incoming data, we have here a helpful description of the moral lethargy, the incurious and unimaginative posture, that speeds the collapse. The overwhelming difficulty of reversing this process, of awakening to ourselves and the call to enlivened and transformed hearts, is not a recent development in human affairs. Millennia ago in one of Jesus's strangest and most challenging sayings, he advises his hearers that it comes down to a question of vision. When the eye, being the lamp of the body, is healthy, your whole body is full of light. When it's impaired? Darkness. The zinger: "See to it, then, that the light within you is not darkness."

Try *that*.

There's a grim moral realism here that's lost when we gloss over the psychic heft of Jesus's hard sayings. The implication here is that we really can (and do) get it *that* wrong, mistaking light for darkness and darkness for light. People who can't imagine themselves as capable of evil are prone to miss this and project the idea of evil on others instead. There's a lot of money and power to be accrued by doing this. Arguably, it's how elections are won. We don't have to succumb to it.

Kurt Vonnegut has another word for us here. Yes, we become what we pretend to be, so we have to be very careful what we pretend to be. But there's a rare and dark admission he left us as a sci-fi writer who was also a veteran of World War II and survivor, as a prisoner of war, of the Allied firebombing of Dresden. Vonnegut had no interest in trying to morally distinguish himself from his alleged enemies, those who, through accident of birth and a received sense of duty, fought as soldiers in the German Army. Here's his testimony: "If I'd been born in Germany, I suppose I would have *been* a Nazi, bopping Jews and Gypsies and Poles around, leaving boots sticking out of snowbanks, warming myself with my secretly virtuous insides. So it goes."[15]

Look at what he does here. He punctures the myth of American innocence at his own expense *and* resists the temptation to lionize his own standing. He opts instead to identify himself as a fellow creature among other souls *also* caught up in the immortality projects of others. By doing this, Vonnegut breaks free of the spirit of self-legitimation—in this case, an easy nationalism well-funded and armed to the teeth—and gives us a gift of discernment and self-deprecation.

I'm amazed by this admission and especially the phrase "secretly virtuous insides." I believe I know the phenomenon well. There's a glossed-over sentimentality, a theoretical love, that, when mistaken for conviction or successfully pretended at for oneself and others, is a form of terror. "Secretly virtuous insides" is a sardonic description of a common occurrence too easily overlooked, woefully unremarked upon, and especially effective when self-applied. Vonnegut's feat of attentiveness to his own interior life invites us to undertake our own.

This is the work of making sure that what you take to be light within you isn't actually darkness, that we aren't fooling ourselves with our speech and our media intake and thereby darkening counsel. The good religion of unlearning the reigning dysfunction we unwittingly inherit and obey isn't something we can pull off overnight. It's an unlearning we're never done doing.

HURRY UP AND MATTER!

Sometimes I look at people and I make myself try and feel them as
more than just a random person walking by.
— Joaquin Phoenix's Theodore Twombly
in Spike Jonze's *Her*

"PRESS 'LIKE' TO HELP JESUS WIN!"

This is the directive that appears on an image that arose on many a
Facebook feed during the run-up to America's presidential election
in 2016. The image features a very white Jesus in a cool, sunlit-valley
setting involving a waterfall reaching across a stone table to clasp the
hand of a horned figure with skin like glowing embers in a hellscape
involving molten lava. The two figures are arm wrestling. There's also
a bit of dialogue above the image:

"SATAN: IF I WIN CLINTON WINS!"
"JESUS: NOT IF I CAN HELP IT!"

It is, in one sense, as silly as can be, but when I place it on a screen in
front of my students, I get looks of weary familiarity. I ask them to

raise their hands if they know anyone they imagine would feel compelled to press "like" as directed. Many indicate that they do. There is something in that which the screen matter proposes that commands a degree of allegiance among millions of Americans. A congressional investigation discovered that this ad was paid for by a Russian account with ties to the Kremlin. The suggestion that religion and politics can be somehow magically held apart in separate stables dissolves upon contact with any sober assessment of how disinformation, in our one human barnyard, works.

Our relationship with our screens is our relationship with ourselves. Social media platforms, like pen, paper, and printing press, can accelerate and amplify what we set down or upload upon them, but tools can't be blamed for what we do with them. Nevertheless, one person's ad revenue is someone else's terror campaign. The Jesus versus Satan image (which invites the viewer to affix the thought of Hillary Clinton to the latter) serves to remind of the stakes in our discourse about ourselves and others, what we let slide, what we abide, what we affirm, what we deny. Are we responsible for the lies we let others voice in our presence unchallenged? There's the matter of safety and setting to consider, but I kind of think we are.

> **Our relationship with our screens is our relationship with ourselves.**

"Mythologies can rule us unless we pierce through them," Adrienne Rich once observed. "We need to criticize them in order to move beyond them."[1] This names the poetic, prophetic, and political task of morally serious people as we try to manage our own psychic dumpster fires and the dumpster fires of others in public. With toxic conceptions of self, God, and others filling up the airwaves, this task can prove very demanding. But as ever, we are not without resources.

Does it feel like it's somehow already too late? Does the thought of getting into it with anyone anywhere feel overwhelming? Is it all too complicated?

Words are all I have. Talk, as ever, is cheap. But this passage sure does lay it out:

> A multitude of causes, unknown to former times, are now acting with a combined force to blunt the discriminating powers of the mind, and unfitting it for all voluntary exertion to reduce it to a state of almost savage torpor. The most effective of these causes are the great national events which are daily taking place, and the increasing accumulation of men in cities, where the uniformity of their occupations produces a craving for extraordinary incident, which the rapid communication of intelligence hourly gratifies.... When I think upon this degrading thirst after outrageous stimulation, I am almost ashamed to have spoken of the feeble effort with which I have endeavored to defeat it.[2]

These are the remarkable words of one man determined to somehow rage against the machinery of mass hypnosis, the general hijacking of the human imagination, and the way we have of fearfully sealing ourselves in informational echo chambers in our self-degrading thirst for stimulation. We might find it heartening to note that this description of a crisis "unknown to former times" was published a decade or so before "The Star-Spangled Banner." The lone resister who penned them? William Wordsworth. And the feeble effort he's undertaken to defeat this degradation of human spirit is his own modest word work. It's poetry he's up to, and he defines it a little famously as "the spontaneous overflow of powerful feeling."

Poetry isn't popularly posited these days as the corrective to our perpetual disquieting or as a habit of mind by which we might get ahold of ourselves. But it is at least that. Have you felt its effects?

Poetry is another person's enlivening testimony, their deep diving so to speak, on your behalf and mine, awakening us to the fact that we live on a planet, that we need not dwell so damagingly upon it, and that the natural world is on our side. It's not an environment after all. It's a neighborhood. Poetry reminds you you're here to enjoy yourself sensually—to experience yourself—as a gift and in the gift of other people.

What we call poetry is our best word for that which makes things new, that which [whispering] aids us in holding everything dear. It's [louder] the spontaneous overflow of powerful feeling [quieter] that takes its origin from emotion recollected in tranquility.

Poetry's a form of behavior too. I can think of people I'd say have been kind enough to *treat* me poetically. One, a teacher listening to me explain what I thought a passage in a novel was getting at, fixed me with a look that said, "I just know you can do better than that." Another, a librarian looking at my account, said, "David Dark. Now that's a writer's name." And a woman in Dublin who'd agreed to house a friend and me for a few nights. As I crossed her threshold, she looked at me a second or two longer than I was accustomed to and said with warm solemnity, "You're welcome." Poetry happens when we're made to really see something previously overlooked, something needful, something that might bring us back to ourselves. I can say of so many things, "That was poetry to me."

If we're to ever be true, if we're to be witnesses to our own existence, poetry speaks in us. With only newsprint to contend with (though the steam locomotive was right around the corner), we can easily conclude that Wordsworth had it easy when it comes to self-presence, hearing your own voice and trying to know where you are and what you're about. If the rush of getting and spending in his own day had him feeling that the mass of humanity was out of tune, unmoved and slowly frittering their souls away with worldly care, we can only imagine what he'd make of the endless distraction in the ubiquitous form of our electronic devices in a frenzied age of everything all of the time.

It's often as if we're witnessing the steady erosion of our ability to have face-to-face conversation, to allow ourselves the luxury of sustained attention to another person's words, to know the sacred pleasure of nuance.

HIGH-TECH HASTE

The prophet of the technological bluff, Jacques Ellul, could not have foreseen the days when agitated people would gaze plaintively into someone's eyes and ask, "Do you have Wi-Fi?" But he demonstrated profound prescience when he observed that a computer isn't a companion; it's a vampire.[3] We are indeed pulled away from others when we gaze into our screens. We become what we do with our tools. But to suggest that hopping on to Twitter, for instance, is always an avoidance of real relationship is to confuse matters and perhaps even project a little.

Twitter amplifies our capacity for the demonic, certainly, but it can also serve as a means to thoughtfulness. It can't be blamed for the content we broadcast through it. If toxicity (degradation, humiliation, bullying) is our primary game, we're able to deliver it remotely and more quickly. It's like the printing press except faster, more widespread, and perhaps longer lasting. Paper and pen, after all, are also social media. And out of the depths of the heart the social media feed speaks. It can be a hellhole, but it can also constitute a profound opportunity for advocacy and amplification. It is what we make of it.

In a wide variety of media, mechanisms of quick and easy gratification are catered and calibrated to play to our fantasies of ourselves even as they leave us diminished and further estranged from the possibility of true, noncommercialized human interaction. Media companies' stock values soar, but we're left with what Stephen King refers to as a "catastrophically fragmented society"[4] in which everyone dreams their dreams alone, often in the darkness of issue silos and increasingly tragically unversed in the mental habits that might make for lived community.

"Every human being is involved in a desperate attempt to narrate himself into a safe place,"[5] novelist Richard Powers once remarked. And what a multi-edged and variously cued dance the social pipeline is. "What's the story here?" we're in so many ways never *not* asking. How do I get *in*? Or, alternately, how do I get *out* of this horrible story? By narrating and *re*narrating away. What is the shape my devotion will take today? What's that voice saying as I reach again for the fire hose of internet one more futile time? *Hurry up and matter!*

Call it an exorcism, if you'd like, or a poetic intervention, or one more witticism by which we can have mercy on ourselves. But "hurry up and matter," a phrase my poet-sage-lady friend, partner in crime and matrimony, Sarah Masen, once offered aloud, has become a saving, clarifying mantra in our household. We have to give voice to the spirit that drives us nuts before we can dismiss it or effectively renounce it. We have many such phrases in our family's attention collection, our everyday liturgy. When I open up my laptop, for instance, she'll occasionally mock me, asking in a child's voice, "Did somebody write me?" Every so often, somebody I really ought to write back right about then *has* written me (or typed me), but the mockery is nevertheless a saving ministry. What am I trying to save myself from when I dip my head again in that current, and where am I hoping to get to? Am I rushing off to *feel* more relevant than the human beings nearby can make me feel? Fleeing the presence of my own presence in a rock-and-roll fantasy? "Hurry up and matter" often seems to name the age, our experience of it anyway, like nothing else. What better phrase is there to name the driving need—or *perceived* need—that takes me straight into the fuel tank of someone else's marketing scheme, away from where I actually am to some deluded, disembodied elsewhere?

GENUINE CONSCIOUSNESS VERSUS TRIVIALIZING SHALLOWNESS

This returns us to the question of what we're up to with our imaginations. And of poetry. And as ever, it isn't a *side* issue because there are no sidelines. What I'm up to with my imagination *is* what I'm up to. It's me *making do*. And—oh so complicatedly—neutrality doesn't appear to be a live option because, as writer Ronald Sukenick said, "If you don't use your own imagination, somebody else is going to use it for you."[6] The question of how I imagine myself and others is at the core of my lived life, how I relate (no getting away from relating), the way I dwell in the world. How shall I go about mattering if *not* mattering isn't an option for anyone anywhere anytime?

Slowly and carefully and with a wary eye on all the flashy, artificial offerings that serve to obscure the reality of where I'm sitting, standing, or walking. There is so much that can call me away from a proper estimation of who I am, where I am, and what the joys of right relation might yet require of me; so much that draws me into a denial of the reality of my own body; so much that drives me to deny, to my everlasting detriment and that of others, the fact of the living world.

As I see it, we most effectively practice the right of dissent and resistance when we decline the given compartments. Consider NFL safety Eric Reid, formerly of the San Francisco 49ers, deciding to kneel during the National Anthem. Consider, too, Vice-President Mike Pence's decision to schedule a Sunday afternoon flight to Indianapolis to publicly shun, on the taxpayers' dime, Reid's Christian witness by exiting the stadium upon seeing him kneeling. We don't do justice to this conflict between a hero of conscience and an elected official behaving like a baptized, white supremacist terror operative if we try to confine this drama to any one news section. Our situation is intersectional. It's a lot of things at once. And to be clear, Mike Pence, who likes to make noise about his generalized faith, is the idolater in this scenario.

Recognizing bad religion when we see it—and it *is* coming at us from every angle—can make us more vigilant and alive to the possibilities of genuine consciousness and more wary of the trivializing shallowness into which we're otherwise unwittingly enlisted. Amid the static that degrades, how might we access wisdom, compassion, hospitality, and other forms of life for which there is no app?

As I see the bad religion situation, the answer isn't a matter of stepping out and starting new traditions so much as it's a matter of approaching the currents we're already in from a different angle, one person, one relationship at a time. And even putting it this way brings to mind the poet-pastor Eugene Peterson, who once observed that the besetting sin of the American people is probably impatience. This sounds right, especially when I consider the possibility that there's hardly a sin that isn't somehow born of misperceived need, of haste and its accompanying inattentiveness, of some feverish variation once more of *hurry up and matter!* Being true—*ringing* true—involves a slow work of recognition and resistance to that nervy, deluding spirit. To begin to be true is to try to choose—or *risk* choosing—presence over progress, *really* showing up and taking the time to wonder what we're really up to, what we're doing and why.

COURTESY OF THE HEART

It will require, in all things, what the poet William Stafford refers to as "courtesy of the heart." He purloins the phrase from Nietzsche as a way of elaborating on the necessity of attentiveness to the minute particulars, bringing in a statement he overheard from a peer in the Civilian Public Service: "I feel that if struck I should give off a clear note where I am. But I don't have to go around beating myself like a gong." Who we are, Stafford understands, will always be enmeshed in the particularities of what we do—and don't do. We owe it to one another—and ourselves—to be as absolutely honest, to give off, as much as we are able, a clear note:

> It's a kind of feeling of wanting to ride the contours of human relations alertly and purely at all times. . . . A person ought to know, not just when you're breaking with them, but when you're enthusiastic and less enthusiastic and a lot less enthusiastic. I mean, it's not just "Everything's fine until it's war." It's a dailiness. I believe it is part of our responsibility to each other. I guess my ideal is a kind of artistic creation and a kind of living, too, in which we enable each other to live by those little signals from now, now, now . . . I think there are these innumerable little nuancy decisions you make . . . all those little revelations of where you are, you know, where your priorities are, and how they might better be. . . . There are a million little signals.[7]

There are, we know all too well, so many ways to miss each other, to even profit in our wicked way—temporarily at least—by making less-than-true impressions in our interactions with people, the easy money and the quick fix of purposefully false signals. It's a popular way of getting by and making a killing, of hurrying up and mattering. And then there's the clear note of nuance, the live risk of candor. Might we try to hold the world with a degree of affection and the openhearted-ness affection enables? What if all the world's a stage and it all turns on affection? Shall we ring true?

A single intake of breath is sufficient to bring us to the admission that trying to ring true is a very messy undertaking. Life comes to us already divided, and in more ways than we can keep track of, we already feel devastatingly compromised. For this reason alone, the divisions feel helpful, almost salvific, a means for getting and staying ahead. I mean, *really*, what *would* we do without them?

But it is also the case that everything we have in the way of ancient wisdom in story and song, whether in Scripture, Shakespeare, or Sanskrit, repeatedly tells us that these divisions are entirely untenable, destructive, and—if it helps to put it this way—even heretical. We're called to pursue the slow and thoughtful work of resisting the haste of false witness despite the cost it might impose. True signals take time.

Courtesy of the heart might be the most countercultural—genuinely revolutionary—move we can make. It's also, obvious to anyone willing to slow down long enough to really think it through, the straightforward task of meeting the basic rule of neighborliness. To risk a hot-button word, courtesy of the heart is even a *conservative* hope, presuming we intend the word literally, because exercising our own powers of reference truly is the first obligation of speech. ("This is that. And that has to do with this. And these two can't actually be rightly separated unless you're . . . you know, trying to sell something. Yourself, for instance.") In our words and our deeds and our deep-down imaginings of people and things, there are so many occasions—once more into the breach!—to try to be true, to begin to really see one another and thereby experience ourselves poetically.

EVERYTHING THAT EVER WAS AVAILABLE FOREVER

While I'd like to us to keep Wordsworth's nineteenth-century jeremiad in mind lest we unduly conclude that we're in *wholly* uncharted territory in the challenge of not losing our minds to technology completely, and keeping before ourselves the possibility of neighborliness and goodwill, I'd nevertheless like us to consider courtesy of the heart despite the flashing lights and siren songs in our midst. Alongside Wordsworth's analysis, let's place novelist William Gibson's take on the state of everyday consciousness for many: "If you're fifteen or so, today, I suspect that you inhabit a sort of endless digital Now, a state of atemporality enabled by our increasingly efficient communal prosthetic memory. I also suspect that you don't know it, because, as anthropologists tell us, one cannot know one's own culture."[8]

What does courtesy of the heart—or even consistency of the heart—look like when the endless digital Now is always only one electronic appliance away, perhaps even interrupting you—now within the space of time it takes to read this sentence? I don't have an answer, but I do have an anecdote. I was standing around talking to people at the conclusion of a house concert looking for reasons not to leave (they were incredibly interesting, my fellow attendees), and we got to talking about a song we wished the artist had included. "Which album is that on?" one of us asked. And the fellow we imagined might know stopped talking and stared into space.

Gesturing toward the device in the guy's front pocket, a friend broke the silence. "You know you could just . . . "

"No," he said, still staring. "I'm doing this the old way."

It was kind of a joke, except kind of not. As good jokes do, it spoke to the mess we're in. He really did access his memories old-school style, eventually recalling the album title and reveling in the fact that he could still do that kind of thing as if, one day, it'll be a kind of party trick. Remember—*remember*—that we can too. Our bodies are real. We can look people in the eye and listen and pay heed and recall things. We can actively treasure, value, and take the time real presence requires. But it involves a determined and deliberate embodiment. We'll often have to *decide* to do it. And we might find that an insistence on presence is something that many a neighbor (young and old) will often find off-putting, annoying, and, given the taskmaster that phony motion is with its *hurry up and matter* alarm system, increasingly inappropriate and unprofessional. Perhaps that anxious future is already here, but it is of course difficult to know your own culture.

If we don't at least occasionally do it "the old way," the avenues for having a proper and functioning attention collection will likely disintegrate. Do hungry hearts still research the names in the liner notes, tracking down the source material of the things they love? Will there remain people in the world, human interest enough, willing to expend something like adequate attention on extraordinary offerings? The old way can begin to feel like the only way cultural treasures might go on *being treasured* by someone somewhere somehow, whether it's reading a book all the way through or placing a needle on vinyl. The slow labor of discovery and the patience real amazement requires are otherwise in danger of being lost.

This is the scenario writer-comedian Patton Oswalt believes places us "on the brink of Etewaf: Everything That Ever Was—Available Forever." As he describes our Etewaf moment, it's akin to the loss of topsoil and the accompanying disappearance of the conditions that make vegetation possible: "The topsoil has been scraped away, forever. . . . In fact, it's been dug up, thrown into the air, and allowed to rain down and coat everyone in a thin gray-brown mist called the Internet."[9] This is a powerfully apt image for articulating the challenge of somehow valuing and receiving—*really* receiving—the witness, the gift of insight, of any and every voice whose carefully rendered creative labor has come to be not just instantaneously ours for the taking, like water from a drinking fountain, but, God forbid, even tiresomely before us like dust we want to wipe off a table.

If what once was treasured now feels disposable, how do we recover or conjure a context for receiving these gifts *as* gifts? Without the giving and receiving of vision—the poetry, the song, the dance that are the currency of Beloved Community—the people will perish. It's as if there's hardly anyone left to actually pick up what's been laid down. And more broadly, how do we recover the gift of one another when there's always one more thing to be distracted but largely unmoved by? Can anyone anywhere get a witness anymore?

If what once was treasured now feels disposable, how do we recover or conjure a context for receiving these gifts *as* gifts?

PEOPLE TAKE TIME

A lived commitment to courtesy of the heart is a revolutionarily sustaining practice. The scope of my attention collection—my own personal canon, as it were—will be determined by who and what I'm willing and open to taking in, the questions and concerns I'll allow to matter to me. This is also where the dailiness of being true will play out in the sounding of a clear note or . . . won't so much. The internet might intensify or quicken this process, making so much of it a part of the global public record in unprecedented ways, but the habits by which we deny ourselves to ourselves and others and those by which we come to consciousness remain essentially the same.

It is indeed a new frontier when someone I haven't seen in over a decade suddenly appears—if it can be called an appearance—to wordlessly post a climate-denial video on what was an otherwise calm and reasoned Facebook thread. But the challenge to try to imagine the person's context and the fact of their desire to somehow be engaged, and to revere, if I may, their attempt to be meaningfully social, is as it's always been. There are, after all, so many who have seen the desire and revered the attempt in me. I will doubtless require their patience again.

People take time. And with a natural sense of awe that drops upon us as if by miracle every so often, we occasionally manage to look upon others with a deep sense of gladness. A recent formulation of this phenomenon comes to us from the character Theodore Twombly, played by Joaquin Phoenix in Spike Jonze's *Her*. Via the kind of earpiece and microphone one can witness in use in cars and on sidewalks whenever you see a person speaking personally into what appears to be thin air, Twombly's pouring his heart out to an operating system endowed with an artificial intelligence with whom he's falling in love. She's christened herself "Samantha," and Twombly's more relaxed and talkative than he's been in months. In the middle of a long night of people-watching, he describes an experiment he likes to undertake: "Sometimes I look at people, and I make myself try and feel them as more than just a random person walking by."

I love his deployment of the word *sometimes*. It's a startling and moving admission that his experience of other human beings as random and generally uninteresting isn't some kind of exception but the norm. In his performance of the duties of recognition, of understanding that there's a unique somebody in each of the bodies passing by, he's only gone so far. But with delight, he notes that he'll sometimes risk the pleasure of trying to see—trying to actually feel—a stranger's presence as something more. It's an expenditure of effort for Twombly, but in the context of this exchange, he speaks as one convinced that it's very much worth it.

NO ONE HAS THEIR MEANING ALONE

As the film proceeds, we're made to see that Twombly has a ways to go. But like a once definitively disappointed child trying to try again, he's ready to recognize and to relish the quandary that is the living fact of other people. It's as if, despite himself, he feels compelled to widen his vision enough to allow another person to mean something that surpasses what he habitually takes them to be. How else can Twombly or any of us place ourselves in the path of beauty or reside in the way of the gift? It's a moment of surrender. This is the way it goes with feelings. And no one gets to have their meaning alone.

This, too, is a courtesy of the heart, that trading of signals whereby we enable one another to live. "Nuancy decisions," Stafford calls them. No right relationship, it seems to me, without nuance. And no nuance until we allow others—ever so gingerly—to tell us what we appear to be up to. As it turns out, I'm not the best

Life's too short to pretend that we already have when we haven't or that we are when we honestly aren't.

or final authority concerning my own meaning. Everyone needs at least one or two people asking them—sometimes begging them—to tell them specifically how they're doing in this unfolding tale of trying to be true. They'll need certain assurances that I'm genuinely seeking their counsel, but people know when you're really asking. It's a commitment to a long and delicate conversation, and it can't be hurried. We get to put the request to folks every so often: "Tell me how I'm doing. Tell me the truth about where you think I am."

Life's too short to not do this.

Life's too short to pretend that we already have when we haven't or that we are when we honestly aren't. There are those who are in an especially good position to tell me the truth because they're the unique recipients of my many assurances and signals, whether clear or purposefully unclear, true or false, my betrayals as well as my promises. My life, if it's to be at all examined, requires their counsel because we are, after all, connected. I am *in* relationship.

Religion is the what, the to whom, and the how of our everyday lives. And the ties are a living fact, non-optional.[10] This word *religion*, carefully considered, names the fact of relationship rather

> **Religion is the what, the to whom, and the how of our everyday lives.**

well, but if it's just too radioactive, too fraught with tragedy and manipulation to be useful to some, it can be let go. I'm not trying to push a word.

But relation—now *there's* a word—can't be consistently denied without loss of life. Life's too short to pretend you're not in relationship or that you're not beholden to someone, many someones, in fact. How do we begin to overcome the widely broadcast distortions, without and within, that insist otherwise and degrade us so? How might we recover ourselves?

6

BE THE RELIGION
YOU WANT TO SEE
IN THE WORLD

*That feeling of a baby's brow against the palm of your hand—how I
have loved this life.*

—John Ames in Marilynne Robinson's *Gilead*

Our pandemic, the Black Lives Matter community, the climate crisis,
the white supremacist terror putsch of January 6, and the #MeToo
movement (which gave rise to the #ChurchToo movement) have
proven to be an existential threat to most predominantly white church
organizations in the United States. For some, what can feel like a disaster might, in time, come to look like a mercifully clarifying moment.
Avenues for seeing, seeking, and joining Beloved Community remain
wide open, but something is being revealed (or shaken loose) when
it comes to our relationship with institutionalized power, which of
course is our relationship with ourselves and the natural world. Our
arrangements *feel* normal until they don't. We become what we abide.
Same as it ever was.

I'm going to put it dramatically: a lot of us are beginning to realize that we've been tied to a network of bigots for most of our lives. Having put it dramatically, let me take it slow: Nobody's just a bigot. Nobody, to my knowledge, *wants* to be a bigot. To love a bigot, if we're in a safe enough position to attempt such a thing, is to love a process. To love a person is to love a process. Same as it ever was.

I have a story about this process. In my late thirties, I went back to school to pursue a PhD in Histories and Critical Theories of Religion. This placed me in class with students sometimes more than a little younger than me. This included undergraduate courses in which I was one of a few graduate students. My favorite was a course in nonviolence, which put me in a room with Reverend James Lawson, the lead activist-architect of the Nashville sit-ins and a lifelong prophet-scholar-practitioner of nonviolent action, for almost three hours each week. I was clocking in time with a living icon.

That said, our time together was sometimes wildly informal. He was eager to communicate that we were each and all invited to the kind of revolutionary self-understanding he represented and that the women and men of the Nonviolent Movement of America, like himself and Diane Nash and John Lewis, were themselves students of others like Lawson's mother, Philane; A. J. Muste; and Howard Thurman. Like Martin Luther King Jr., Lawson felt a peculiar debt to the witness of Howard Thurman. He asked us to raise our hands if we knew or had heard of Thurman's book *Jesus and the Disinherited*.

I so wanted to say I had, but I hadn't. I felt a degree of relief when I noticed that hardly anyone else in the room had either. My relief was short-lived.

"I'm about to say something nasty," Rev. Lawson said. "Most of you don't know about Howard Thurman because most of you are white."

Ouch. I didn't like how these words made me feel, but I'd been given a few seconds of warning, and I knew he was right. This incoming data could not be easily denied. I had not been called a bigot to my face, but I was being shown something about my own media diet up till then. It was needlessly deficient. Why not sit with it? Why not linger in the fact of this realization for a moment before reacting? Perhaps there's insight on the other side of shame.

There was, and there is. Lawson had a lot to show all of us in the classroom. He believes our nation is awash in the myth of restorative violence. Against the suggestion that what we have in the way of civilization (infrastructure, the rule of law, the Bill of Rights) we owe to those who fought, killed, and died to secure it, he believes we owe it to those who might have taken up arms against those who uphold our criminally unjust system but chose and choose instead to confront it nonviolently. We owe it, then and now and over the millennia, to the embodied practice of Beloved Community.

Lawson also makes distinctions I've never forgotten. He admires and learns from Mahatma Gandhi. But he differs with Gandhi, who maintained that he had no enemies. Lawson explained that he does have enemies and defined an enemy as someone who's so estranged from their own moral power that they are practically wired or calibrated—through fear, shame, projection, and undealt-with trauma—to do damage to people they find in their path and over whom they are accorded power. He offered an example one evening: "George W. Bush is my enemy."

"But," he quickly added, "Jesus instructs me to love my enemy." Here, too, I was being schooled. Is it possible to love a person while also recognizing, as a matter of candor and conscience, that they are, at least for now, locked into speech and behavior that are a danger to themselves and others? Of course it is. In Lawson's presence, profoundly demanding realism and profoundly demanding optimism coincide.

He recently brought it to his analysis of the Black Lives Matter movement. By his reckoning, it isn't merely the latest iteration of the work he's undertaken his whole lifelong; it's actually an improvement.

It is succeeding in ways it didn't and perhaps couldn't in the twentieth century. It's more than a protest. It's a spiritual act of public worship:

> They have organized around the grief and offered a ministry to the families of the Black men and women who have been shot and killed by the police. They have helped those families to grieve, helped them to be empowered—to not let the murder, the execution of their child, go quietly away. . . . They have surrounded almost every family with a ministry of healing. . . . They are saying [of the use of extrajudicial force and killing] "This is not God's will." To me that is astounding and it is happening in our society today. The movement is calling for the dismantling of the old forms of racist violence that we have taken for granted and replacing them with new forms of kinship that will allow us to be a far stronger nation and better people. Repent of the sin and take on new life, that is a Christian and religious mantra.[1]

These are the forms of life I'm eager to enter and by which I'm determined to measure myself. New forms of kinship come into view when I take in Lawson's words and try to imagine the world as he sees it. Beloved Community, in this sense, affords us a lens for better apprehending and responding to friend and alleged foe alike, to see and sense kinship everywhere and somewhere in particular.

I want people to feel their own moral power. I want membership—of the most human-thriving sort—I long for church, but it's complicated. Church attendance? I don't actually think such a thing is possible. It could be either the neurosis or the wisdom at work—that I've trained my children to speak of the place to which we sometimes drive together on Sundays as a church *building*.

We've been known to attend the *meeting* of the church, we might say. But I want to get the words right. I want to keep us all in the way of the gift. I want my family to think of their people as a mobile assemblage of folks we know and are coming to know, dead and alive and still to come, who are uniquely committed to the living out of neighborliness and conviviality and justice. And it's incredibly important to me that they not confuse these people and their living relationship (the membership and dedication to Beloved Community) to them with any institutional structure or [face in hands] building.

Will Campbell, who mentored and worked alongside James Lawson and fought for desegregated schools and lunch counters while also seeking relationship with incarcerated Klansmen, asserted that *church* is a verb, a peopled activity that, in one sense, ends when an institution (or a building) begins. I want my children to think of being *in church* as being a collective witness of fellow human beings, wherever they are and whatever they're up to—that is in the middle of a living work of art.

The Nones,[2] the supposedly "religiously unaffiliated" who make up roughly one-fifth of the American public (one-third of adults under thirty), are also part of our collective. I see Earthseed in the Nones and Dones. And an interfaith future, a people uniquely interested in *not* unthinkingly drinking the proffered Kool-Aid and inspiringly aware of the dangers of doing so. Faced with the question of "present religion," one can be forgiven—or maybe even congratulated—for looking over some of the options (Protestant, Roman Catholic, Jewish, Muslim, Hindu, atheist, humanist) and initially seeing bigotry and boundaries. Aren't these divisions part of the problem? Why the one but not the other? Buddhist but in no way agnostic? Protestantism cut off from Catholicism *and* Judaism? Might there be lines of continuity among the multiple-choice "answers"? Can we believe more than one thing? Can I see myself as something of a hybrid or perhaps write in an affiliation with the Jedi?

Aren't we all made up of a wide variety of influences (like the proffered affiliations themselves)? Too easy an identification with one affiliation to the exclusion of the other feels like the same sad, dysfunctional song of too many a century. The labels we claim are conveniences that only ring partially true—if at all—and never tell the whole story. Beyond whatever boundaries we presume into existence, why credit these divisions? It's more complicated than a casual circling can say. And an unexamined religion is not religion worth having.

We are each the sum of many affiliations, many perceived necessities, more than anyone can possibly keep track of. As much as we might be prone to love our labels as ourselves, the idea that anyone is ever only formed by a single religious tradition is a central fallacy of our time. We are, in fact, all hybrid now as we enter an inescapably interfaith future. Contrary to the suggestion that Millennials live plugged-in lives with thinner relational networks or are less invested in advocacy and justice, I spy people who long deeply for the real deal, who are committed to operating more critically concerning the suffering produced by being plugged in unthinkingly to any number of things, and who are eager to live and think more nimbly in view of the realizations afforded us by the large and small apocalypses on offer amid our climate crisis, our pandemic, and the white supremacist terror putsch of January 6. The question of what truly serves human thriving, of what work is and isn't essential, is ever before us. When I consider the foodies and food trucks, the artisan backlash that has so many of my former students diving into woodwork, pottery, and all manner of sustainability, I'm challenged, inspired, and deeply encouraged.

The moral movements fused with and leading up to our pandemic have shown us something. We're beginning to see anew that we become what we sit still for and that the reigning arrangements are arbitrary. I see people running *toward* a deeper awareness of relationship, not from it, people *more* alert and alive to the ways we have of depleting our own value, not less. *True religion.* Let us count the ways we long for it in song and dance and getting and spending. Those who wave their freak flags at festivals or decide to have song lyrics, a phrase from Shakespeare, or a Wendell Berry quotation tattooed on an arm have not, to my mind, lost the plot; they're looking to become more meaningfully invested and knowingly situated *in* it, in spite of its daily elusiveness. They're looking to expand—not close—their circles of sympathy. What else is a lifetime for? More and more are wonderfully willing to risk getting caught believing in something.

YOU HAVE A BODY. JUST ADMIT IT.

I'm heartened by these phenomena because they strike me as instances of people deciding for positive obsession, for owning their own enthusiasms in a more embodied way. They are one step in the lifework of seeing what we're scared of, deeply acknowledging what we're hoping for, and no longer living in defensive denial of our own raw vulnerability. The absolute importance of leveling with ourselves concerning our sacred desire to be a part *of* something (so easily exploited and perversely applied) instead of standing apart *from* everything and everyone (as strong and in control as that makes us feel) is at the heart of my plea that we rethink our positions in regard to what we call religion. Because we are mutually caught up in the life of the rest of the world in all that we say, do, and consume, there are disavowals that don't stand up to scrutiny. To decree "I'm spiritual but not religious," as religion writer Phyllis Tickle reminds us, can be a little like saying "I'm human but not flesh and bone." I, too, have a body, a body that needs things, does things, and pursues them in particular ways. It is by way of my own perceived necessity that I participate and am, in fact, implicated in the lives of others. To think I'm capable of opting out— or to honestly believe I've done so with a bored shrug—is to miss an opportunity for a more embodied sense of myself in relation to others.

It's disconcerting to try to have a conversation with people who speak as if they don't possess a particular point of view, but this habit is legion among us. It isn't only other people, we are pushed to admit, who live within a context.

When we really admit to the fact of our own context, we're less prone to deny others the complications of their own, making empathy a living possibility. In this sense, the good news about weird religious backgrounds is that we all have one, and there are as many as there are people. Numbering ourselves *among* those who conduct their lives according to strange ideas about the world, acting out one form of devotion after another, whether inspired or ill-conceived, means refusing to keep ourselves aloof from the rest of humanity and accepting a place among our fellow pilgrims also searching for meaning, also trying to make sense of their own lives, and also living with the difficult and pressing question of what to do in light of what we know. We begin to take up the task of empathy when we're susceptible to the sense that the inner lives of others might be as real and as realistic as our own.

The *feeling* of disconnectedness from what someone else believes is a fact that gives us something interesting and even wonderful to talk about. But to claim or insinuate disconnection *as* a fact, as if we've extracted ourselves from the social world, the labor and patience of others upon whom our livelihoods depend, is to live in delusion and denial. The more difficult and excellent way is to live without

The good news about weird religious backgrounds is that we all have one.

alibis and without succumbing to the tired temptation to front with one another, to concretely own up to also being situated so that I see my life as morally answerable to the people around me. I don't believe I can even begin to do this as long as I honestly think I can sidestep the question of religion because it is precisely nothing less than the question of my own devotion. Needless to say, *religious* devotion, like a religious value, a religious priority, or a religious ritual, is hopeless redundancy.

Religion, after all, is nothing if not relationship, the way I go about relating to the world made plainly evident by the forms my relating takes. And relationship, like culture, is non-optional. I'm always cultivating and relating in one way or another, whether generously or mercilessly, whether with care and caution or in a pinched, fearful, endlessly defensive fashion.

Like any relationship, religion can be very bad, but it can also be very good. It can be true, and it can be devastatingly false, this way we have of dealing, coping, and managing with ourselves and others. In this sense, the question of religion is always the question of right relationship, a question that can't be justly avoided by anyone anywhere. Even when we try, it's a question that comes to us in our dreams.

To reference a figure within the dark depths of the Marvel Universe, right religion will always depend on what we do or fail to do with what Steve Ditko's Doctor Stephen Strange once referred to as "the basic power of the imagination." Everything turns upon it, swaying us to the mood of what we like or loathe. An early Strange tale featured the good doctor performing acts of saving wizardry on behalf of the inhabitants of a village in the Bavarian Alps possessed by hostile spirits from another dimension. In his final standoff with an incorporeal being that had overcome the mind of the village's hapless mayor, Strange responds to the poltergeist's final taunt with an overpowering spell: "There is no power greater than that which I possess, for mine is the basic power of the imagination, the gossamer threads of which dreams are woven."[3]

What we weave and, more disturbingly, what we find woven around us in binding images, ideas, and stories about the way the world works is ultimately decisive in the way we conduct ourselves, what we fear, bet on, and hope for in all we do. When our imagination is transformed, culture follows, and when it has hardened past the point of yielding to insight, we the people perish. Whether it's a trap or a means of transport, the tangled web of what we're able to imagine, the meanings we assign and design in the spaces we're in, defines our lives. And our capacity for illusion is limitless.

As counterintuitive as it might seem, the essential ethical task of being a part of where I live, of being a body meaningfully present among and to my family and surrounding community, is one with the work of imagination. Right livelihood begins with right conception, and because I can't easily conceive the web of relationships out of which, say, an affordable cup of coffee is placed before me, I am compelled to try to imagine it as justly and realistically as I can. To *see* truly in spite of all that I can't *know*, I have to try to *imagine*. No neighborliness, we might say, without a careful and far-reaching imagination—reaching beyond, for instance, the question of how inexpensive the coffee is for me and toward the lengthy liturgy involving those who grew, cultivated, and picked the beans and hopefully own the land on which they labored. So much depends on where we go with our imaginations.

INESCAPABLE NETWORK OF MUTUALITY

When I'm overwhelmed by the dominant and dominating version—or perversion—of reality that would cut us all down to the size of caricature and "use value," I'm blinded to all manner of righteous possibility in my daily existence and largely robbed of the beautifully complex presence of others as they are of mine.

That we're tied up with one another is a fact. An unrelated person, like an unworded word, is an impossible thing. How we address the fact of our relatedness is the perpetual question of what we do with our own self-understanding, our own voices, our own vocations. "Who is my neighbor?" is perhaps the most political question imaginable. Thinking of the question as religious (as well as political) helps me to scrutinize those parts of my life that would otherwise too easily escape my attention.

I have in mind here Martin Luther King Jr.'s phrase in the Birmingham epistle, words that invite us to see ourselves more realistically and responsibly by recognizing that our lives are caught up and sustained within an "inescapable network of mutuality." No unrelated people. No isolated facts. Everything we do or neglect to do counts when we allow ourselves to be "cognizant of the interrelatedness of all communities and states."4 King's vision isn't simply a beautiful picture but rather a summons to moral seriousness, a breakthrough if we'll let it be, and a challenge to see ourselves as members of one another and, by doing so, to remember well in the way we esteem our fellow human beings near and far. The deep realism to which he invites us to orient our thinking and doing is the deep relatedness against which national boundaries, ethnic divisions, and class structures appear as the consensual fictions they ultimately are. Do we have the eyes and wit to perceive as much? Do we want to?

To see truly is to see seriously. The Buddhist monk Thich Nhat Hanh offered a quick beginners' course in doing so in his consideration of the source material and the human resourcefulness hidden within a single sheet of paper. Holding one up, he asks us what we see. Paper? Yes, but what else? Hanh invites us to look harder by imagining more: "If you are a poet, you will see clearly that there is a cloud floating in this sheet of paper."5

In an awareness of process, we see that a cloud has to be there as we recall the fact that a tree requires rain. There's also the sun. There's a lumberjack present too *and* what the lumberjack had for breakfast that tree-felling morning *and* the farms on which the items in that breakfast were produced. We also might notice the lumberjack's parents. To begin to imagine these connections—and again, they don't require our imagining or our awareness to be living facts— through the living fact of interrelation is to begin to imagine with sacred nuance. Far from being an escape into disembodied bliss or fancy, this sensibility dissolves whatever dichotomies might keep us from perceiving and responding to the complex relatedness of all of life. It is a call to a deeper investment in the given world than our usual ways of construing the world allow. And lest we miss the call by referring to Hanh's teaching as a *spiritual* perspective concerning a piece of paper, please note that Hanh and King and their ilk are inviting us to think more realistically, not less. Answering the call to consciousness begins with the determination to be realistic by being awake to the everyday liturgies we personally undertake as well as those of others, the liturgies of other people upon whom our own lives depend.

If I'm to be a person of *good* faith, each day is an occasion to imagine with greater accuracy and appreciation the net, the latticework, in which I'm caught up, the labor out of which my life has been made possible, and to experience the fact of my relatedness as a gift and a responsibility. To conduct my life in *bad* faith is to proceed in denial of this relatedness in speech, action, and investment. The avenues for proceeding in bad faith are myriad and multiplying, often appearing before us as the only means for, as the saying goes, *getting ahead.*

What I do with a strange phrase like *getting ahead* will depend on how I go about imagining my own context. What's forward and what's backward? Who do I hope to get ahead of, and where do I imagine I'm getting *to*, exactly? Does it include playing well with others? Do I resent even being made to ask these questions?

DUMPSTER FIRE

At the height of our COVID-19 pandemic in Tennessee, I was shopping at a grocery store when I heard shouting and then witnessed a white man dressed in camouflage threaten to kill someone who'd asked him to put on a mask. He followed the death threat with this: "It's been a hell of a year!" That observation, obviously, didn't excuse or change the fact that he'd threatened to kill someone in public, but it did offer an impromptu narration of how he might have wished bystanders would interpret his actions, a play for sympathy.

That part at the end got me thinking about projection and boundaries and evoked, for me, a teaching from the gospels concerning Gehenna. *Gehenna* is sometimes translated as "hell." Lately I've seen it can be helpfully read as a description of a psychic state common to human beings that is both figurative and, when made manifest through action, literal. In this sense, *Gehenna* can be helpfully rendered as *dumpster fire*, with which we can name all manner of dysfunction made plain in word, action, image, and output.

In the unmasked man's refusal to don a mask when asked I spy a dumpster fire. But I also feel a degree of compassion for him, considering the likelihood that the difficulty he had controlling it is contact traceable to someone else's difficulty controlling theirs. Jesus's difficult teaching concerning gouging out eyeballs, cutting off hands, and drowning oneself instead of violating a child is, as I see it, about managing your own dumpster fire instead of terrorizing someone else with it. We are each liable, at times, to project our own chaos on others as a way of asserting a sense of control. What we do with our struggle is what we will have done with our lives. But the greater war, we are instructed, is the *inner* one. That's where the true work gets done.

Preventative self-harm, Jesus grimly notes, is preferable to initiating a new cycle of trauma *if* you're unwilling to seek the help you need to not hurt other people. Consider the acronym THUG LIFE

("The hate you give little infants f***s everybody") placed before us by Tupac Shakur. The hate, the dumpster fire, within has to be worked out creatively and nonviolently. Addressing a man in camouflage or a friend or a family member concerning their abusive behavior risks triggering them. But the call of good faith often involves risk.

Taking on that risk is a form of loving candor. It's the same loving candor I trust my children will exercise with me should I prove to be in the grip of militant ignorance, my dumpster fire, which I cannot see without the assistance of others. The risk is infinitely preferable to pretending that I can't see, smell, and sense the dumpster fire to which friends, family, strangers with and without guns, and my elected officials have succumbed when they speak and act in such a way that I know they are, at least for now, unhinged and unsafe. We owe it to each other to say what we see. To love a person is to love a process. [*points at self*] We have to mind the dumpster fire within and without.

We have resources for addressing our inner conflicts. In what I hope might be called good faith, I seek the finer tales of who we are and what we're up to, those creative offerings—it could be a moment in a pop song—which seem to place reality, even if only for a few fleeting seconds, in a truer perspective, reviving and directing me toward the fact of where I am.

I have available to me, for instance, Marilynne Robinson's John Ames of *Gilead*, who knows something about our inescapable network of mutuality—think *way of the gift*—and the joys and the duties of right reverence when holding someone's life in your hands. He describes holding an infant as follows:

> While I was holding her, she opened her eyes. I know she didn't really study my face. Memory can make a thing seem to have been much more than it was. But I know she did look right into my eyes. That is something . . . I realize there is nothing more

astonishing than a human face. . . . You feel your obligation to a child when you have seen it and held it. Any human face is a claim on you, because you can't help but understand the singularity of it, the courage and loneliness of it. But this is truest of the face of an infant. I consider that to be one kind of vision, as mystical as any.[5]

In *every face* a claim. There is so much here to summon us to reverence, to prompt us to ask what in hell we think we mean when we tell ourselves we're on the verge of getting ahead. Ames knows that the mind plays tricks, but he is compelled to brood on the stewardship of astonishment, of learning and responding to the beauty at work in any human face. An entire doctrine of the sacred exists in this short passage on living, seeing, and knowing artfully in which Ames seamlessly unites ethics with aesthetics and compassion. How could we forget that they're one?

PREEMPTIVE SYMPATHY

The courage and loneliness of another person's face draws on me and claims me because *I cannot help but understand* their singular relation to my own. I'm called to see myself within their vision, to begin to see myself as they might see me, and the resulting vision is indeed mystical because so much remains concealed in the fact of communion, that space in which we experience ourselves as undeniably related, as kindred, knowing it all a joy. To be in communion with others is to recognize that I can't be myself to myself without imagining them well and therefore justly. Again, the question of art, the question of how and what I imagine is everything.

As I understand him, Ames is describing what the mad farmer-poet Wendell Berry refers to as "preemptive sympathy," that task of attentiveness by which we begin to "recognize with sympathy the fellow members, human and nonhuman, with whom we share our place." It isn't a once-for-all achievement so much as a habit we find ourselves taking up or tragically putting aside many times a day. Some form of preemptive sympathy is a prerequisite of good faith, which, for Berry, achieves visible, words-made-flesh form in the occurrence of affection: "As imagination enables sympathy, sympathy enables affection. And it is in affection that we find the possibility of a neighborly, kind, and conserving economy."[6]

I love it when Wendell Berry speaks of conserving things because the mere thought of him reminds me of all the ways a radioactive word like *conservative* might still be properly sounded with a sense of due heft. I enjoy telling my students that I'd never risk the presumption and hubris of calling myself *conservative* because such an assessment could only *maybe* be appropriate at the conclusion of my life, made by people in a position to make that call.

What did I manage to conserve and share for the good of whose commonwealth?

Was my life a tale of neighborliness or largely one of fear and defensiveness?

What did I really do with what affection I had?

These questions are sobering, and they enliven me. They center me, even as they make me feel the poverty of so much of what I do and say when I ignore them. The good news is that, at any moment, I can change the story I'm telling myself. And in its appeal to my imagination, the kingdom of God might be said to come little by little, one recognition at a time. Wendell Berry suggests that we might free this sacred vision of its sectarian associations, as well as our own tendency to assume we already know all about it, by referring to the kingdom of God as the Great Economy. It's that sacred vision of a membership that excludes nothing and no one and within which everything we do or don't do signifies.[7] Such sacred visions beckon me to turn my imagination back toward the human circle, to locate my existence within it and to ask myself how far I'll allow my sympathy to reach, to remember despite the fact of a culture that often appears hell-bent on dismembering our understanding of ourselves at every turn. What might it mean to seek first the Great Economy?

The good news is that, at any moment, I can change the story I'm telling myself.

TRUE RELIGION

If my religion is my relationship to the world, good religion would be the work of developing, growing, and deepening consciousness, not closed, shut, settled, rigid, or done for but one of ever-unfolding receptivity and, if you like, continual repentance, a continual turning away from all of my not-quite-worthy-of-life commitments, a way of taking responsibility for what I do. In this sense, it seems to me that owning this relationship *as* religion is a requirement of good faith and therefore a step in the direction of true religion. Bad faith begins in the disavowal that will own up to little or nothing. And in turn, bad religion is the disavowal of relationship, a denial made plain in any practice we have for dividing ourselves from others, those ways we have of turning away from the fact of kinship.

One such practice, peculiarly predominant and damaging in the activities of our westernizing world, is the rhetorical strategy that only keeps the concept of religion at a distance, as if we've magically removed ourselves from the complexities of relationship. When we're enmeshed in bad religion, we have a way of denying the fact of our own bodies and degrading and destroying the bodies of others. Oversimplification kills. It always has.

Good religion cherishes bodies, and it is evident in any practice that restores, reinforces, reconsiders, and redeems the human form, locating it, in Thoreau's phrase, as a part and parcel of nature. Good religion is at work in the cultivation of consciousness and in all that involves us in seeing ourselves truly, in experiencing ourselves—and helping others experience themselves—anew. We know it when we see it, and we learn it, necessarily, by heart.

We risk falling into deluding abstraction if we take the matter further and speak too knowingly or boastfully of *true* religion. But lest we grow too abstract in our thinking about such a thing, a very helpful text attributed to James, the brother of Jesus of Nazareth, maintains that one sure sign of true religion would be the lived concern for orphans and dispossessed women.[8] When we think of it this way, we're invited to view at least one indication of true religion as plainly discernible among pockets of people the world over, people united in spite of a wide variety of confessions (including atheism).

Admittedly, this straightforwardly humble standard for crediting one another as sound can frustrate those of us—our number is legion—who tend to place the litmus test for faithfulness in the realm of what we *say* we believe about God or life after death or who should be accorded the legal right to marriage, but the modestly on-the-ground work of being good to people often proves to be a scandal to our egos. And the criteria for actual neighborliness, especially toward the vulnerable, remains eye-rubbingly clear most of the time. The demands of true love are almost scandalously obvious and much more demanding than saying or trying to convince others we believe certain impossible-to-prove things.[9]

The criteria for actual neighborliness, especially toward the vulnerable, remains eye-rubbingly clear most of the time.

The love that is true—that love against which there is no legitimate law—is much more commonplace than we're prone to recognize if we're regularly informed by the hysterical talking points of those who profit (or believe they profit) from stoking the fires of fear and resentment in our vision of those who appear bitterly foreign to us in a zero-sum game of a world.

There are better ways of viewing those souls whose names we find it difficult to spell and pronounce, human faces by whom we won't be moved or astonished so long as we're willingly enlisted into narratives of bitterness and diminishment when it comes to our fellow humans. Though they might not get any screen time, every day blessed people, here, there, and everywhere, hunger and thirst for good, committed to taking care of the otherwise disinherited among us (which, apart from certain infrastructures available to some but not to all, is *any* one of us at so many points in our lives) and longing for a future in which everyone has what they need to thrive. There are solid people everywhere, it turns out. True religion springs eternal every once in a while.

It springs whenever we're awakened by a vision of ourselves as wonderfully and undeniably bound to others within the beauty, the darkness, and the complexity of what I refer to as the Verse, that sanity-restoring colloquialism for the visible universe I borrow from the interplanetary culture of the *Firefly* series. Removing the *uni* (*unus* is Latin for "one"), *Firefly*'s far-flung space pilgrims in the future see the totality of existence (*versum*—a rotation, a row, a turning) as a process of change. When we speak of the Verse, we draw on a humble but imaginative posture that envisions what we feel we know of reality—the felt truth of a "known universe" we have to see feelingly to see at all—as a kind of row that human consciousness hoes as well as it can in its discerning of worlds in flux. Like "as far as I know" or "I can only imagine," it asserts the fallibility of the speaker who might otherwise be understood as speaking too knowingly.

Because awakening and embodiment go together, ubuntu is the knowledge out of which arises the practices of generosity, hospitality, and compassion that *say*—as only actions can—"my humanity is caught up, is inextricably bound up, in yours." We see most feelingly that "we belong in a bundle of life" and that "a person is a person through other persons." In welcome tension with the estranging emphasis on individual identity we associate with Cartesian dualism ("I think, therefore I am"), ubuntu asserts, "I am human because I belong. I participate, I share." To have a sense of ubuntu restored is to experience oneself connected again. "A person with *Ubuntu* is open and available to others, affirming of others, does not feel threatened that others are able and good," said Tutu, "he or she has a proper self-assurance that comes from knowing that he or she belongs in a greater whole and is diminished when others are humiliated or diminished, when others are tortured or oppressed, or treated as if they were less than they are. . . . To forgive [in this sense] is not just to be altruistic. It is the best form of self-interest."[10]

That feeling of known belonging is the literacy of how to be—and know oneself to be—together with people. And it is a literacy we never stop learning, a literacy of wonder. In my efforts to lift up the ancient vision of ubuntu as a standard in my own mind and to commend it to others, characterizing it as a *religious* vision serves no helpful end at all. For one thing, I don't think it's possible for a vision to *not* be religious, and for another, decreeing it religious only makes it easier for many a contemporary mind to reject it with all the weird and bitterly anxious divisions of self from others such a rejection makes inevitable.

But the question of religion, the way we relate to the world, falsely, truly, badly, or healthily, remains before us. And I believe it is most profoundly addressed when we see it as indistinguishable from the question of membership. Of what whole do I perceive or know myself to be a member when I place my hand on the brow of a baby or a child or even a full-grown human? If I feel myself awash in love of the life I share with the sometimes courageous and sometimes lonely face of my fellow member with whom I've exchanged this intimacy, will I proceed accordingly? Will I live up to the claims of my intense recognitions, or will I detach myself in the hope of achieving something more secure? A *maximizing* of my position?

There are so many ways to lose a right sense of ourselves amid the demands and the perceived have-tos of our unbalanced and misperceiving world. But I can discover and reclaim my own membership anew at any time by way of the dignity and creativity I witness and feel with others. I can bring what gifts I have to the flow of a gift economy upon which we've all along depended one more time, holding out my attention collection with open hands in expectation of receiving, once again, an education. I can recover the plot by leveling with myself concerning what I'm up to in my expenditure of energy and what it is I mean to do with my one wild and precious life, as Mary Oliver writes.

And again, it's a work that's never exactly done, but it's also as straightforward as artfully recovering a kind of self-presence. Søren Kierkegaard describes it as a process we get to take up repeatedly if we're to receive a sense of our own context: "I should suppose that education was the curriculum one had to run through in order to catch up with oneself."[11] The curriculum comes to us through the attentive care of others, whether in lyric, image, conversation, poem, remembrance, or a well-timed, open-ended question, and it is indeed geared toward a literacy of loving well. As Tutu tells us, this is the love that is actually self-interest at its poetic best. As that commonsensical paradox characteristic of the ubuntu insight has it, it is only by really loving and forgiving others *as members of ourselves* that we can begin to really love, forgive, or cherish ourselves at all.

7

THE CHOTHER

In the prophets, we note that "the world" is never generic; it is one's own world.
  —Daniel Berrigan, *Jeremiah: The World, the Wound of God*

Because so much in my life is a return to the attention collection, I have a concept, sacred in my estimation, that arose from repeatedly leaving a child alone in front of a television. It's a serendipitous slip of the tongue I gleaned and now treasure from the testimony of my once-four-year-old son when he offered a commentary upon an iconic image within the Hanna-Barbera tradition. Giving voice to his specific love for the antics and escapades of Scooby-Doo and the community with whom he makes his way through a harried world, my son once told me that he especially likes the moments in which Scooby and Shaggy get scared to the point of paralysis. In what I suspect is a touchstone in every episode, though I can't claim to have studied the matter thoroughly, there comes a time when Scooby and Shaggy respond to duress (a man in a monster costume, for instance) by leaping into one another's arms and quivering together for a couple of seconds, a precious moment in which it's hard to say where the dog stops and the man begins. They hold *each other*, we might say, but in his effort to articulate what delighted him so, the child put it much, much better: "They hold their 'chother."

With the enunciation of this concept, that of *the chother*, I believe we're sitting squarely within the glow of a religious insight, an insight that meets all manner of resistance—*also* religious—in our hurry-up-and-matter, mad, mad world. First, the resistance. As I understand it, the idea that any of us can have our meaning alone or be the sole authors of our own significance or have joy for which we only have ourselves to thank is a death-dealing delusion. This psycho covenant implies, for instance, that a strong, successful few might somehow gain their lives without losing them, that there are those who have *earned, thought,* or *bought* their way beyond the neediness—the essential vulnerabilities—of relationship. And as the delusion has it, there are those among us who through will, drive, and ingenuity might somehow join them. Influencers? VIPs? High-impact people? You know the parlance, the creeds.

THE MOVEMENT OF ANTI-GRACE

This bizarre and ineluctably religious vision of humanity in Western-world popular thinking viewed simply as *the way things work,* it's awfully difficult to hold it at an angle different enough to consider the possibility that it might not be so.

Pull yourself up by your own bootstraps, the saying goes, as if such a thing were possible. *Hard work pays off.* Well, of course. Yes. It *sometimes* does. Does this mean that anyone who isn't getting paid is in that pickle for lack of trying? Or that those who do get paid—and then some—have what they have for having labored so truly and excellently? *That* would be an insane claim. And it's *so* in circulation, a myth perpetuated among adults like a handshake, a tale told to children as if it were gospel, a contagion we know to be very much airborne.

Begin to see this bizarre religious vision, and you'll see it everywhere; it's the default moral of a very significant chunk of the best-selling contemporary tales of our time on display at the airport. Is it not the case that a sizable sum of the stories on offer give a moving account—you can skip to the end—of how someone hurried up and at long last mattered? Why are those faces on those magazines? These are the amazing people who finally got it together and really went for it. [eyes closed] All hail the power of the lone individual.

There are so many ways of naming this popular delusion. It's the very hubris that gets classically played out in song and story and on screen and stage repeatedly, and it's probably remembered and then quickly forgotten as a problem we ourselves might have numerous times on any given day.

One very helpful naming of the evil spirit comes to us from the mind of writer George Monbiot, who gives to this otherwise airy nothing a local habitation and a name by describing and skewering the phenomenon as *the self-attribution fallacy*. Perhaps you've witnessed it: "This means crediting yourself with outcomes for which you weren't responsible." Ever discerned that little mind dance in action?

Think of self-attribution as the movement of anti-grace. It's the opposite of the way of the gift. This isn't to say that we bear no responsibility for any positive outcome. It's just that the conditions for thriving so many of us enjoy aren't *necessarily*, um, all rooted in justice, we might say. An awful lot of what we have—clothes, computers, food, the abode in which we lay our heads to rest—arrives via "the ruthless exploitation of others and accidents of birth." Or in some cases, to put it more simply, "luck and brutality."

Where I come from, many are fond of recalling aloud that they don't deserve what we have, a cliché that doesn't always go especially deep in our self-understanding. Nor does it play out in the way we like to see the lives of others ordered. Not so much. Because this is all a "myth of election" so easily reduced to comedy the moment a sober person comes close to voicing it aloud, it can only thrive—and it really does—through insinuation and the explaining away of the lived tragedies of so many whose access to abundant life is blocked by the wicked ordering of life and resources we anxiously lobby to keep in place. Monbiot brings the whole house of cards down with this analogy: "If wealth was the inevitable result of hard work and enterprise, every woman in Africa would be a millionaire."[1] Self-respect? Certainly. Love your neighbor as you love yourself? Of course. Self-attribution? If that one has hold of you, you may as well claim the demon's name that's possessed you. In fact, you kind of already have. Watch what happens when the teleprompter breaks.

IN THE BEGINNING WAS RELATIONSHIP

Scooby and Shaggy, meanwhile, hold their chother. The wondrous image is of course just one more iteration of the ancient, soul-savingly obvious but *still countercultural* realization that to be whole is to be part. If we hold to the chother principle, we understand again what we're hell-bent on denying and forgetting, that our very sustenance and whatever identity we can be said to have come to us via the fact of relatedness or not at all. Just look at that social pipeline. Ubuntu. Because we can see that there's a kindness, a sweetness, that immediately follows the insight—that *is* the insight—that my own life can't be ultimately divided from the lives of others or even defined at all except *by way* of others, *our chother*. I am because *we are*. Or as the Jewish mystic Martin Buber liked to say, in the beginning was relationship. Whether via the biblical injunction to die in order to live or the Buddhist principle of *anatta* (no self), all manner of ancient wisdom counsels that whatever self I can be said to have is the gift of self I receive from my relation to others, the groundless ground (think of the way Shag and Scoob almost levitate) of the chother.

The realization of the social fact of the chother happens all the time. The hope that it might happen today, some lived experience of real community, is often what gets us out of bed in the morning. And of course, in what can be a slightly sad way, it's why we retreat to another screen. It's why we eavesdrop, and it's why we like to sit in bars and coffee shops. It's the way we look to a song. We ache for it. When we're confronted with crisis, when we join together in music, or when we experience (or receive) a vision of soul, whatever the source, the question of where my one life starts and that of my neighbor stops begins to dissolve, and the bad, sad-making religion of hyperindividualism takes on an unreal and unseemly quality. By way of our chother, we begin to discern our true position in a fuller picture of the world we're in. We were never really able to take it all in by our lonesome anyway. It takes two to see.

In such moments, we're summoned not so much to act *as if* the road to life, loveliness, salvation, and sane seeing can only be entered into where two or more are gathered but rather to proceed in recognition of this sweet, scandalous, sometimes embarrassing fact. For one mad moment, we're relieved of the sociopathic burden of trying to convince ourselves and others we're self-made people who might matter just a little bit more than the average human. We get to give that heavy defensiveness up (deep down, we desperately hoped to anyway). We get to find, hold on, *and* let go within the circle of each other— our chother.

Life's too short to be lived in a swirl of perceived self-attribution, anxiously resistant to the grace that is the fact of the matter. All those little distancings add up after a while till we're too debilitatingly detached from reality to meaningfully see ourselves beautifully at all.

The vision of the chother challenges us to relinquish that distancing reflex, to let go of that fear, and to access a baseline recognition of kinship in others. *All* others. Numerous pilgrims, we come to realize, have been here before.

THEY ARE NOT "THEY"

In Louisville, Kentucky, there's a street corner with a sign commemorating one such everyday apocalypse. It's the spot on Fourth and Muhammad Ali (formerly Walnut) where the monk-writer Thomas Merton claimed to have experienced a laugh-out-loud epiphany in which he found it strangely and suddenly impossible to view passing strangers as at all random, uninteresting, or, in any lasting way, separate from himself: "I was suddenly overwhelmed with the realization that I loved all those people, that they were mine and I theirs, that we could not be alien to one another even though we were total strangers. It was like waking from a dream of separateness, of spurious self-isolation." With chothers, properly considered, there is no hierarchy. "The whole illusion of a separate holy existence is a dream."

Even as a monk, Merton found he too easily fell, years at a time by his own admission, for the sham of separateness. Even a life *set* apart—however it is we play at such illusions—can never ultimately *be* apart. "If only everybody could realize this! But it cannot be explained." His vocation to solitude, as he came to understand it, was not an escape from human communion but a means to accessing, knowing, and feeling it more deeply: "It is because I am one with them that I owe it to them to be alone, and when I am alone, they are not 'they' but my own self. There are no strangers! . . . If only we could see each other that way all the time." If only, but an insight can't be explained any more than it can be enforced. Like an ethic or a witness, it can only be, as it were, stumbled into, fallen upon, and, in the way of the gift, received.

For all its profundity, the Louisville epiphany is an easier yoke, a lighter burden, than the wicked dream of self-attribution. Deliverance from the illusory difference—the positing of a *mine* that is forever and in no way *yours*—is a most serious relief, a relief that can turn the whole world around. Merton equates it with the overcoming of evil with good: "If only they could all see themselves as they really are. There would be no more war, no more hatred, no more cruelty, no more greed.... I suppose the big problem would be that we would fall down and worship each other."

In Merton's vision, like the vision of the great commandment, the false distinction between love of neighbor and love of self is collapsed. There is ultimately no such thing as a nonsocial self. It appears to be a work of accessing that part of us that *isn't* divided from others, that we somehow know *can't* be. It can't be proven or preached. Only testified to, witnessed, and proffered as a way of seeing. Only felt: "I have no program for this seeing. It is only given. But the gate of heaven is everywhere."[2]

COMPLEX REMINDINGS

Never one for flights of disembodied fancy, Merton—it seems to me—isn't spiritualizing everything so much as he's including everything in whatever we believe we've contained or cordoned off with the word *spiritual*. Consider it this way in the words of Merton's fellow Kentuckian Wendell Berry: "The context of love is the world."[3] Here, Berry drops an aphorism so plainly true yet so plainly revolutionary as to merit a tattoo. The love you carry in your heart is largely delusional till it puts on flesh. It simply has to. It requires a context to exist. It can't survive as theory or fantasy. It has to step out. It's the chother or nothing at all.

Love requires a neighborhood.

My big ideas, my alleged virtues and values, and my supposed integrity will have to be played out in the blessedly difficult, mundane sacred of where I am. This realization is lost on me repeatedly as I fall again into a dream of separateness. But I'm awakened and restored to a sense of my situatedness by all manner of what Berry calls complex remindings,[4] at the center of which are experiences relayed and remembered, the images, words, and analogies that make for poetry. Poetry deepens and renews my discernment of the beauty and fragility of my context—its dearness—and assures me once more that there's no escape from it. There's no outside, we might say, to the social pipeline, but poetry is that which orients me back to the joy of dwelling rightly and righteously within it, that which reminds me I'm always within it one way or another.

There's an urgency to this coming alive—or coming alive *again*—to the fact of relation, and it's captured profoundly in a centering provocation of Hillel the Elder: "If I am not for myself, who will be for me? But if I am only for myself, who am I? If not now, when?"[5] It's as if we're being accosted by a two-millennia-old wit that knows—then *and* now—that all our deadly, self-attribution pouting is a kind of delay tactic of intensely unhelpful and even murderous denial.

What am I? And who can ever reach me in my closed-up loneliness if I keep kidding myself with a false image of an isolated, self-sufficient self? I can't even *help* myself. We can fool ourselves. And we do. That which often passes for civilization and society is, in fact, ordered and organized around this delay tactic. But the rabbi calls us—and a prophetic tradition calls *through* him—to forget this house of cards. It's a farce. We can die trying, and we do. But we *cannot be* alien to one another.

The chother is the fact of the matter. We were never alone. We were all held as babies *by others*. We're likely being held—in more ways than we can even name—right now. We can live into and within the awkward-feeling fact of others, or we can die denying. Choose the chother now. Know it feelingly. Choose life. If not now, when?

MUST. LET. GO.

As if the world needs more of the delusional and desperate dance in which we try to keep up appearances, I have a story that speaks to this subject. It isn't completely flattering.

I was in San Diego impersonating—very badly—a surfer. I was completely hopeless. At the most, I could claim five solid seconds standing solidly on the board. The rest was all saltwater of the beloved Pacific, in and out of my nose for hours on end. A generous onlooker, however, might nevertheless have seen in me the signs of an excellent father. I'd swim out with my youngest son, Peter (sacred articulator of the chother principle), and offer shivering screams of support. I'd push his board—sometimes expertly on time—in anticipation of the breaking wave that would engulf me before I could recover enough to witness his totally awesome progress. No absentee parent, I.

Except I almost was absent in what was, for me, a humiliatingly definitive sense. The ritual whereby I'd cry out affirmation as we returned to each other to venture out again was interrupted by the realization that I was suddenly too far out to see or even call out to him. And with each wave, however hard I tried to plant my feet in the sand to stop moving or swim briskly and competently to the shore, I was being pulled out farther, becoming more exhausted, wondering if my movements were slipping into a panic mode (as I now know they were). And—most surprisingly to me at the time—I was preparing to let go of my sense of composure, which, I came to see, was peculiarly sacred to me. Oh, how I cling to composure. *Must let go.* Surprisingly, and even disturbingly, I experienced a moment in which I wondered if I was going to let go of that composure, a second or two in which

I actually weighed it out. I decided I would rather live having lost it than die keeping it. To name one soul who came to mind, I owed as much to my chother, my brother, my son.

Don't be ridiculous, I said to myself. You need help.

"I think I need some help over here," I yelled to a nearby surfer (I *think* I need? God help me). He obliged and allowed me to clutch his board as I tried to catch my breath ("I think I just . . . need a minute"). Missing waves he wished he were catching, he rebuffed my pathetic efforts at small talk. In hindsight, I can understand his annoyance as I asked—oh so pathetically—if he was from the area.

"Here comes the lifeguard," he mumbled, disappearing without one word further as my young, able-bodied savior hugged me with a flotation device. It gets

Don't be ridiculous, I said to myself. You need help.

worse. Safe in my lifeguard's arms, I tried to kick a little, the better to somehow self-reassuringly carry—or appear to carry—my own weight.

"It's probably best if you just stay still," he observed politely as we took another wave together. Per regulation, it seems, he wasn't going to take the floatie off till we were both standing on the shore in plain view of everyone. Because he was off searching for me elsewhere, my son was spared the sight of his no longer indomitable dad trying to thank someone for saving his life while also looking to distance and disassociate himself as speedily as possible.

"Where were you?" he asked with wide-eyed alarm when we finally found each other.

"Have a seat on the towel," I said. "We need to talk."

WHAT'S THE MYTH?

I'm still contemplating my complex reminding. Something in my conception of myself, I believe I can say, was irretrievably—or maybe a little more definitively—undone. And it wasn't just the fantasy that, in a pinch, my stamina will somehow magically conquer any and every obstacle, that a deep adrenaline reserve will kick in so I'll have no need of anyone. It's as if a myth I thought had no hold on me to begin with—I read Wendell Berry and Thich Nhat Hanh, for God's sake—was now *really* no longer available to me. I thought I was over it. I wasn't. And—God help me—I'm not. Trying to process the experience with my daughter Dorothy a day or two later, she asked the obvious question: "What's the myth?"

I couldn't sum it up in a sentence, but it was as if I could feel my own body repenting of a certain thoughtlessness and my mind was trying to catch up with it (it still is). I was shaken, but something within me wanted to make the most of it. If I explained it away too soon, I'd lose access to the information my shame and frustration and bodily humiliation might have for me. I didn't want to regain my lost composure just yet. What's the myth? The nearest example of one hidden but powerful mythology at work involved some excellently prepared chicken my daughter and I had recently shared upon purchasing it at a nearby farmer's market that day. I could start there.

There's a way of describing that particular exchange that goes like this: We paid for it with our money. So we're square. The end.

Having just had my life saved by a couple of strangers, I felt weirdly uninclined to accept that version of a recent event. It was just one more iteration of what we might call the reigning religious faith of the Western world, a uniquely unbeautiful myth, one in which the cessation of relationship occurs—split, divided, exhausted, conquered, over and done—when *I* say it does, when *I* think it's finished. This cuts the world down to the size of my smallest self. Reducing the care of the chicken, the life of the chicken, the preparation of one part of a meal, the labor and care of the people behind it, and our enjoyment of the whole situation to the exchange of one form of alleged currency felt somehow awkward and inappropriate. I didn't want to think that way anymore. In the wake of the waves that almost drowned me, I found I honestly couldn't. What a waste of time self-deception is. And to regularly insist that *this* can be reduced to *that*, in all the exchanges that make up a day, began to feel like life lived as a sort of smear campaign, life lived one *hurry-up-and matter*, one degrading myth too far. What if God, not bypassing the chother, remembers everything money makes us forget?[6] Maybe we can try to too.

A SAVING MEMORANDUM

Why not err on the side of the relational? Why not repent of all the insidiously goofy ways we try to keep realization of community at a distance? Life's too short not to. Our life is one long process of mutual aid, and what a relief it is when people act on this knowledge.

The fact of the chother frees us to spy the possibilities of undivided living, living marked by deep integrity and humility in its root sense (*humus*, earth) of *knowingly* earth-bound life, situated and connected to the existence of everyone else, not detached, disincarnated, or, in any sense, above it all but grounded in the joys of conscious relationship. How might I proceed in my getting and doing while holding—or being held by—the realization that everything that lives is holy, life delighting in life?

The insight of my—*our*—life as chother comes to me as one more saving *memorandum* (Latin for "something we will do well to remember") that protects me from the deluding abstractions that would otherwise leave me estranged, one more item of cosmic plainspeak we can add to the sacred inventory that gives our speech sense to begin with. Sensible speech eschews abstraction and intensely attends to the minute particulars. Art, science, and other forms of human thriving—Blake again—have nowhere to really happen, nowhere to exist save in minutely organized particulars at large somewhere.

The nowhere talk of general good is the abstracting plea of scoundrels, hypocrites, and flatterers. All the little distancings of generalized and commercialized life that estrange me from my neighbors—and they from me—can add up in the course of the day, distorting my self-perception so powerfully that I'm largely immunized to wisdom.

Against these perverse mental processes underlying our perverse speech, the Jesuit priest-poet Daniel Berrigan recalls that, for the prophets, there are no generalized, contextless visions because ideas can only live in people and places and things. The prophets enact, demand, and invite us to join them—as they always do—in a subtler perception of the sweet old world.

> In the prophets, we note that "the world" is never generic; it is one's own world. It is the slow cohering over long time of a culture; friends and family and land and language and dance and song; a world of coherence and beauty, each element infinitely precious, irreplaceable. Thus "the world," a cohesion of beauty and truth and joy, makes sense, wins the heart, becomes one's own—as a dance does, a poem, a work of art. (Especially for children, that "world" in all its fragility is to be cherished and guarded, a nest in which coherence, truth, and tenderness are honored.)[7]

Oh, how we're prone to flee—in mind and body—a lived realization of the fact of our own nestedness. And what damage we wreak by doing so. The context of life and love *is* the world. Until we experience it as such, our energies know no rest and we have yet to make our home, our neighborhood, our own.

But as ever, nobody can force us to feel ourselves bound by beauty to the duty of seeing ourselves inextricably and blessedly tied to one another in all things. There can be no compulsion, after all, in religion.

A lived celebration of awareness can't be coerced upon anyone. We can't exactly be made to see ourselves in others or enter into that more direct unity of the chother. But it could be that, until we do, we have yet to assume our full humanity. I think here of Ralph Ellison's *Invisible Man*, whose narrator offers his own singular experience as one Black man in a world ordered according to the rules of white supremacy in the hope that the reader might somehow sense their own voice in a tale candidly told, a social pipeline overlooked a countless times, now made visible. Radically openhanded telling true, he imagines, is probably his only possible method and his only hope. "What else could I do? What else but try to tell you what was really happening when your eyes were looking through?" asks the Invisible Man. Maybe we *will* see. Perhaps a call is being successfully transmitted: "Who knows but that, on the lower frequencies, I speak for you?"[8]

With this question a table is set and a site is made ready and available for all takers. Perhaps the form of life I've tried to conjure here shall *inform* yours. Maybe it's been happening all along. And more, perhaps we aren't merely being addressed, spoken *to*; maybe we even feel we've been spoken *for*. Perhaps we hear our own voice lifted somehow within the voices of others. If not now, when?

8

POLICY IS LITURGY WRIT LARGE

How did we get so morally strange?

—Teju Cole

I once had a morally strange exchange, and it went something like this.

I stood in a driveway with the pastor of a large congregation making small talk while keeping a watchful eye on children skateboarding. There was a lull.

"I'm an advocate," he said, breaking the silence. "Wait—that's not the word." I waited for the word. "I believe in climate change," he said starting again, and I agreed that one would not want to self-identify as an advocate of climate change. "I believe in climate change, but if I told my congregation, they'd probably tar and feather me." Silence. "I guess that makes me a silent prophet."

My head began to spin. Prophets, we might say, are many things, but silence is not in the job description. You don't get to studiously steer clear of upsetting the wrong people in all circumstances and claim the status. You can't sound a clear note and mislead simultaneously. I tried a few lines out in my spinning head: Perhaps we should pray together that a witness might arise from within your congregation. Is it right to drive around listening to National Public Radio (NPR) while rolling your eyes over what parishioners might say if they knew you were listening to NPR? Maybe they could handle it. Maybe they're counting on you to tell them things they won't like, things they aren't hearing from anyone else they feel they can trust. Isn't there another adjective for the prophet who's silent? Is *false* the word we're looking for?

I didn't say any of these things. But the lava flowed within my heart for days. Doubtless self-righteous, indignant, I rambled it all off to another pastor. He smiled and dropped a helpful word on me: "Well, I guess *you* were a silent prophet then."

Compassionately skewered, it took me an embarrassingly long while, but I came to conclude that my silent prophet pastor was paying me a deep compliment. Why would he say something like that to me? Why would he entrust me with the airing out of that unflattering self-assessment?

Maybe for the same reason I set myself up to get knocked down a few days later.

If, as ancient authority has it, we are somehow each person in our dreams, maybe something like an unconscious desire to overcome estrangement is at work in the things we say without knowing why. Given what he took to be my commitments (I am, you can see by now, a talker), my pastor friend was actually kind enough to wonder what I might have to say to the fact he has yet to share his conviction concerning the future of the planet with his congregants who— sometimes aggressively—don't. Every spoken word is an act of faith, after all. But I stood there. And missed my cue, missing the fact of my nearby chother asking for a little input. Judging felt easier and stronger than empathy. It never is.

What do we owe each other? Observational candor at least. When we're safe, I think we owe each other as much truth spoken aloud as our nervous systems can handle. Do we need to get into it with everyone? Probably not. We each only have so much bandwidth, so much breath, so many heartbeats. And yet the threats facing us are intersectional. A pastor, pundit, or politician who feels they can't afford to begin to level with their peers about our planet *or* the right of human beings to love and marry whomever they want *or* white supremacist terror *or* the outlawing the discussion of history, thought, and contemplation through the banning of efforts like critical race theory isn't left with much to talk about. One thing has to do with another. Yes to community, commonality, and unity. But listen: a call for unity with abusive people is a call for more abuse.

That last one implicates me too. Let me say it again: a call for unity with abusive people—and those of us who enable abusive people—is a call for more abuse. The personal is political, and our conflict avoidance costs us everything. We become what we coddle, and the ignorant bliss I abide among people I'm in relationship with isn't bliss for the victims of our ignorance. Intersectionality means noticing—and insisting—that one thing has to do with another. Many of the people who want to outlaw the teaching of Black history also deny we're cooking the planet also push patriarchy also bully trans youth also defer to a white supremacist sexual predator who tried to overthrow our government. Is it any wonder *intersectionality* is a word that unsettles the powers that be? Nevertheless, it's time to risk speaking and acting upon the light it shines on our preferred abstractions.

Bearing witness is a complicated business. So many compromises we make in the space of one day. So many opportunities to drop the ball of being true. So many supposedly solid reasons to live just short of full disclosure in our communications with people (associates? friends? sisters? brothers? congregants?) who might be surprised to hear how unsafe we presume they'd prove to be should we do something as radical as, say, make the fullness of our alleged convictions known.

Dare we attempt courtesy of the heart in our everyday dealings?

Do we dare, in the parlance of gambling, show our hands?

If our vocation, our deepest calling, is to ring true, and if our witness is the sum of everything we do, we might begin to conclude that life's too short not to.

Yes, it's complicated, but maybe we owe it to our chother to come out of hiding. Why must we front with one another? Every ancient prophecy assures us *truth will out* anyway. And yes, it's hard to understand something when our paycheck depends on not understanding it, but what does it profit a prophet to gain a world of popular credibility and forfeit the plainly true? It's always been a hard pill to swallow, but what else are gospel, prophecy, and poetry for? For freedom. Another day, another opportunity to repent of idolatrous thinking. Another chance to convert and to come clean. This is the long conversion only relationship—a deep awareness of the chother—can nurture. This is the call to poetic awareness, to the nonreactive heart and the nonduality of Beloved Community, of seeing myself in conscious kinship with others.

> **Why must we front with one another? Every ancient prophecy assures us *truth will out* anyway.**

Maybe we owe it to our chother to come out of hiding as often as possible.

To be whole is to be part. None of us gets to have our meaning alone. We can't ultimately escape the living fact of our relationship to others. At our best, we know it and celebrate it instead of denying it recognition, the way our postures and power drives make us think we have to. Or as the mystic practitioner of public broadcasting, Fred Rogers, once put it, as if calling to us from an alternate universe, "We are intimately related. May we never even pretend that we are not." But pretend we do, and our pretense costs the whole of creation dearly. True religion necessitates the showing of hands, and when we don't, we do endless damage to every minute particular. Love's labor's lost again and again.

The silences that surround the fact of global warming, the everyday social tragedy we bankroll in our soul-flaying commitment to mass incarceration, and the human sacrifices we exact under the banner of our supposed security aren't random; they're orchestrated. To borrow Octavia Butler's phrase, we are the ordinary people who fund and underwrite the monstrous things our society sanctions as legal and proper. What we call "the economy" isn't inevitable. It isn't fate. The ugly ordering of people and resources is an arrangement from which we can withdraw our consent, in big and small ways, at any time. Time to go granular or go home.

"The revolt against brutality begins," writes Rebecca Solnit, "with a revolt against the language that hides that brutality."[1] This helpful aphorism concerned with the way we harmfully hide ourselves with words and the speech habits that roll in and out of the mental habits points to often perverse ordering of bodies, communities, and resources. The words of Jesus point to this as well—it's the way we speak that defiles us. To conceive of religion under the dictation of popular headlines is to conceive it incoherently. To perceive it as somehow separate from the whole of human behavior is to hide from ourselves.

Newspeak touts "the role of religion," people *getting* religion, "religious issues," or the presence of a "religious aspect" in the interest of presenting a "religious angle." But this is like saying—as if it were a compellingly interesting news item—that "relationship was a factor," "language played a role," or "culture was involved." The fact is it's always already there. It can't suddenly enter the picture. We can't get past religion any more than we can live without communal ties, societies, stories, or symbols. It's what we're up to. It is, in so many ways, the human subject.

We're always consecrating in one way or another, and our religion—if it's to be true, if it's to be faithful, life-giving, and responsible to the possibility of life—will have to assume a form of openhandedness, a relentless willingness to change my posture in light of incoming data, a welcoming of the counter-testimony, the differing experience of others. This calls for a certain nimbleness. Pluralism, after all, isn't a problem to be solved. It's an opportunity for receiving the witness, the beauty, of others. And again, beauty prepares the heart for justice.

> We can't get past religion any more than we can live without communal ties, societies, stories, or symbols. It's what we're up to. It is, in so many ways, the human subject.

MYTHING PERSONS

Like our religion (always hybrid, always a mixed bag), our liturgy (*leitourgia*, which can perhaps be helpfully defined as the work of the people) is never more or less than what we actually do with our energies. And when we try to divide up the world in such a way that a suicide bombing is *religiously* motivated but the crowd killing of alleged anonymous militants in a drone strike, for instance, is borne of the *always reasonable* demands of national security, we leave dysfunctional orderings of human life, the bad religion we underwrite with our getting and spending, our voting, our tax dollars, and our consuming unchallenged. We let ourselves off the hook when we imagine we can keep any behavior outside of the sphere of our religious commitments, the stories to which we pledge our allegiance whether consciously or unconsciously with everything we do and don't do. All religion—repeat after me if you're willing and able—all the time. All religion, all the time.

All religion, all the time.

This returns us to the question of our attention collections as the way our specific lives specifically play out in an attention economy, the everyday liturgies we perpetuate in the minute particulars. If religion names the ordering of our priorities, what miracles might come when we begin to pay attention to ourselves? What conversions might wakefulness require? If, as *myth*ing persons, we never outgrow our need for a coherent account, a better story of what we've experienced and what we're up to, how might we tell *and live* a better one, one more intensely concerned with and responsive to the life of the world? How might we live divided no longer?

We begin by exercising certain duties of resistance when it comes to the stories we sponsor and sustain.

We begin by exercising certain duties of resistance when it comes to the stories we sponsor and sustain—they're religions, after all—when we go with the flow to the detriment of our world, our neighborhood, and to the detriment of other people living and yet to be born. There is no moment in which you are not mattering, belonging in one way or another, living up to or in general contempt of any number of narrow or incredibly broad traditions. It is sometimes said that it's the narrower ones that lead to life. How's your traditioning coming along? Whatever the currents are that move you, they're flowing—it's perhaps helpful to observe—right now. Your religion is the story you tell yourself about yourself to others. As it happens, it doesn't always coincide with what we think—or say—we believe.

Will it turn out that you belonged mostly uncritically and unthinkingly to a particular cultural context? Did you wrestle with it, or was your life one of automatic obedience, a series of unfortunate events in which you carefully ascertained what values you were expected to appear to have from one moment to the next and dutifully did so, aping along as it were along the path of least resistance? Were you, in large part, a silent prophet?

BAD RELIGION BREAKS THE WORLD

Like worship, liturgy, and other forms of perceived necessity, it seems to me that there is no off switch in these matters. Here again, *witness* is the word that serves to overcome the reigning dichotomies into nonbinary feeling, thinking, and seeing. One hears tell of worldviews, values-voters, and generalized faith ("man of faith," "faith-based," "faith-driven"). Faith in what, exactly? When we speak of witness, we slow the tape on the raw feed of all we're up to as individuals, communities, countries, and those combined collective efforts of extraction, sales, and consent called corporations. For better or worse, our witness—the values we actually embody, *not* the values we say we have or try to *advertise* ourselves as having—is glaringly, sometimes crushingly obvious.

All day long, nonstop, we value and devalue people, places, things, and the possibility of arable land and potable water for the babies to come. "What shall I make my witness today?" we get to ask ourselves each morning. What minute particulars will I fix my attention upon? Who and what do I mean to love well? Your gift to the world might be answering these questions well from time to time, pulling this one off in your own small way with your own set of sensitivities and enthusiasms, taking the measure of your own attention span, which is, of course, a kind of prayer. To ring true, to sound your one clear note with your one life, might it be appropriate to kind of think of it as something like your duty, dharma, or the word of the divine to you?

If it's right to say that my witness is made publicly available in all that I say and do, I begin to see that I have more avenues for faithfulness, for life and liveliness, than the conventional dividing up of reality allows for. I have a couple of aphorisms I find it helpful to keep in front of me as I try to overcome the false dichotomies coming at me in every form of teleprompter, damaging dualisms that, unless I resist them, I find deeply imprinted in my thinking, my speech, and my everyday imagination.

The first is from the ancient writer Irenaeus of Lyon: The glory of God is a human being fully alive.

The second is my own: Policy is liturgy writ large.

These two aphorisms problematize—righteously problematize?—all manner of issues, certainly more than I can count. But at the risk of inspiring issue fatigue, I'd like us to consider some questions they generate: What might we gain if we begin to consider climate change, immigration, healthcare, gun law, waste disposal, foreign policy, and the right to clean water as ineluctably religious issues? What do we lose when we refuse to? If we refuse to recognize our own religiosity, our own complicity, in the living out of very bad ideas about the world, our costly complacency goes unchecked. We need not look too far to see and know—feelingly know—the ways our bad religion breaks the world. We dwell in the fact of its establishment. We always have.

To the issue of government-sponsored terror—whether involving Muslims tortured, detained, and killed without trial; the escalation of drone strikes, or, in Charles Krauthammer's perverse phrase, "telegenically dead";[2] the denial of Palestinian land and human rights—the novelist Teju Cole once raised an especially poignant plea: "How did we get so morally strange?"[3] While I imagine there's no end to possible responses to this colossal question, the one with the most gravitational pull in my thinking is the popular bracketing off of religion—faith, liturgy, common life—from the violence our society normalizes in the name of perceived necessity. True religion knows no neat divisions. The more we divide, the less we see.

EVERYDAY IDOLATRIES

"I was in danger of verbalizing my moral impulses out of existence."[4] Anybody know the feeling? These are the words of one of my favorite realists in the world. In a wonderfully specific way, they name the danger we're all in, but they were uttered in the context of a criminal trial by Daniel Berrigan.

We heard from Father Berrigan in the preceding chapter concerning a prophetic understanding of the world—the world God loves; the world that is our home; the world for which we are, all of us, in so many ways responsible; the world that is our gift, our inheritance, and our trust. As a poet and a priest, he views the cosmos as a space in which there are no unrelated phenomena and tries to live accordingly. And like so many in our beleaguered times, Berrigan is involved in a mental struggle, a moral improvisation when it comes to the question of how to dwell redemptively in an age gone mad, an age largely in thrall to the social dictates of, in awkward mouthful, the military-industrial-entertainment-incarceration complex. Berrigan consistently describes the dysfunction wrought by all manner of misconceived human self, more poetically: "Immortal urges do not come cheap, whether in lives or resources."[5]

In the course of his long life, Berrigan served for and within many a community of discernment around the world as an intellectually lyrical presence in speaking justly to power and figuring out what faithfulness looks like in the shadow of our reigning geopolitical liturgies of domination and degradation. While he's clearly felt the pinch in different ways throughout the decades, the season in which he articulated this concern over verbalizing his moral impulses into nonexistence was at the height of the Vietnam War in the late '6os. His brother and Josephite priest Philip Berrigan, a combat veteran of World War II whom civil rights activist Stokely Carmichael once described as "the only white man who knows where it's at,"[6] had been involved in various direct actions throughout the era, but Daniel had mostly expressed opposition to the war in classrooms and in writing. For both Berrigans, the extent to which the alleged leadership of faith communities throughout North America had obediently lined up to support uncritically the US government's endless military escalation had given rise to a vocational crisis. Where was the witness to justice, to the words of Jesus? As Daniel put the question:

> Who owned the tradition, anyway; and who was worthy to speak on its behalf? . . . Indeed, the issue was not simply that a tradition was traduced daily by those responsible for its purity and truth. The issue was a far more serious one. . . . The tradition was a precious voice, a presence, a Person. The war had silenced the voice, outlawed the Person. Church and state had agreed, as they inevitably did in time of war, that the Person was out of fashion, "for the duration." He had nothing to offer in the face of guns. . . . He was a prisoner of war this Jesus. He was in a species of protective custody.[7]

What were these priests to do when so many in their own communities had largely reduced themselves to radio silence, to supporting the idolatrous ordering of the nation-state? They would bring the liturgical forms with which they'd been entrusted by their tradition to the war-making liturgies, the paperwork, for instance, of the US government, whose enlisting of young men to commit acts of indiscriminate violence and devastation upon the people and the land of Vietnam constituted, according to their understanding of Scripture, a demonic stronghold.

Following weeks of prayer and discussion, on May 17, 1968, they joined seven other activists and walked into a draft board in Catonsville, Maryland; removed papers with the names of men scheduled to be conscripted; and conducted the prayerful burning of draft files with homemade napalm. Apologizing for their fracture of what they could no longer abide as "good order," and noting that they were no longer able to say "peace, peace" when there is no peace, they observed that they thought it fitting to burn paper instead of children: "We could not, so help us God, do otherwise." As the fire burned, they punctuated this purposeful ritual by reciting the Lord's Prayer.

They viewed their action as a redemptive raid on the *sacrosanct*. And a moment's reflection on that almost excruciatingly helpful adjective—*sacrosanct*—is a reminder that it is indeed *ever in play*: borders, weapons facilities, private property, bodies, laptops, art installations, automobiles, wildlife preserves, smartphones, paper money, documents, designated areas. Choose your own liturgy? We do. All the time. And the Catonsville Nine did one fine day: "Those draft files! They were, of course, more than they purported to be. They had an aura, they were secular-sacred documents of the highest import."[8] They chose to be militantly transparent—maybe life's too short not to—when it counted. And in this way, their *transparent* liturgy would serve to disrupt and destabilize, even if only in one neighborly instance, the *unacknowledged* liturgy of the draft.

Were they wrong to do so? Our answer will largely depend on our sense of the sacrosanct. What's yours? Take your time on that one; it's difficult to discern the content of your own religion. But it's worth finding out.

THE ACTUAL WORLD IS OUR ONLY WORLD

What did the Catonsville Nine accomplish? They were imprisoned, their faces were placed on the cover of *Time* magazine, their criminalized behavior was a *palpable hit* in the sense that it *made the news* for a time. Similar actions they and others undertook and which continue into our day, often under the moniker of the Plowshares Movement, pose, as the prophetic always does, the question of authority.

To whom and what are we rightly *subject*?

What shall we *credit*? How shall we *adhere*?

To what are we *devoted*?

Like any prophets in any era we care to name, the Catonsville Nine confronted and dramatized the reigning dysfunction of their day in one specific and costly way. By confronting and dramatizing American liturgy at home and abroad, the action sought to provoke a meaning crisis for the American public, positing a sacred sense of reality counter to reigning disorder, making plain the brutal arbitrariness of "the way things are," creating scenes of recognition in which the habitual devaluing of life is no longer deemed inevitable, necessary, or even realistic. As Daniel Berrigan modestly puts it, the poor mortal is to go ahead in spite of all:

> I tried, in response, to put matters biblically. That there was a history for acts such as ours. In such biblical acts, results, outcome, benefits, are unknown, totally obscure. The acts are at variance with good manners and behavior. Worse, they are plainly illegal. More yet: everything of prudence and good sense points to the uselessness and ineffectiveness of such acts. . . . And yet, and yet, it is also said: The poor mortal is to go ahead; in spite of all. To go ahead, in faith; which is to say, because so commanded. . . . One had very little to go on; and

went ahead nonetheless. Still, the "little," I reflected ruefully, had at least one advantage. One was free to concentrate on the act itself, without regard to its reception in the world. Free also to concentrate on moral preparation, consistency, conscience. Looked at in this light, the "little" appeared irreducible, a treasure. . . . So, despite all, a history of sorts was launched on a May morning in 1968. Also, a tradition was vindicated, at least to a degree. Or so I believe to this day.[9]

So many evocative phrases to challenge religious thinking. Among them, "very little to go on" brings to mind W. H. Auden's everlasting take on the paradoxical power of the poetic, which makes nothing *happen* and yet survives somehow in the valley of having been said, which is its own way of happening, a way of happening that might be "little" and precise enough to change everything. In this case, the seemingly small gesture was, for the Berrigans, nothing less than the vindication *in time*, the public coherence outside one federal building in 1968, of the biblical tradition itself. Nine supposed nobodies gave witness to it in the space of minutes, speaking the truth in love one more time, standing by the jams, the redemption songs of millennia.

The popular news cycle paid heed within hours, but one on-the-scene verification came immediately from a local FBI agent who, upon seeing Philip, exclaimed, "Him again! Good God, I'm changing my religion!" The liturgical clarification had gotten through. As Daniel saw it, "I could think of no greater tribute to my brother."[10]

The frustrated FBI officer is not alone in his confusion. Isn't religion supposed to stay out of politics? Isn't all that deeply comforting church mumbo jumbo all about the next life? Against that best-selling false witness of otherworldly consolation detracting from the witness of *now*, Berrigan posits that the prophetic vision is one in which "the actual world is our only world"[11] and insists that divinity must be understood as operative in the this-worldly, reality-based realm. Berrigan's witness insists that *now* is the new *then*: "Humankind, it seems, has always been overdue to see God's Word as subversive of a human dis-order largely disobedient, rebellious, and perverted—one close to self-destruction from toxic fouling of our nest, or from weapons designed to protect our *mammon*, the money of exploitation. The word of God revolutionizes this social chaos nonviolently, replacing the politics of greed, blood lust, and violence with politics designed for children."[12]

And with this appeal to A. J. Muste's famous demand—still largely unmet—for a foreign policy dedicated to the healthy thriving of children, the pervasive moral strangeness we breathe and normalize with our everyday acquiescence is once again brought to light. Then as now, we forget so easily. Like so much human goodness, the Berrigan witness often seems to have been forgotten or repressed. But mention the names of Daniel and Philip Berrigan to American men of a certain age, you'll see a light go on in their faces as if they're waking from a dream or recollecting a moment of clarity that once resonated most decisively before life moved on. They're the men who once waited to see when their number might come up. Many went overseas, and some stayed in school to avoid the draft, found employment that would exempt them, fled the country, or, as is the case with more than a few, watched certain strings get pulled to keep them out of harm's way.

They remember those priests who practiced religion by throwing a wrench in the machinery of death, by bearing witness to a universal and transcendent life in a dark time. For a good many people, it was a very big deal. Including David Byrne of the Talking Heads, who believed it to be a godsend. A Maryland resident at the time, he once mused that his own name was likely among those listed in that sacrosanct paperwork made to go up in smoke.[13] He remains thankful for the way those nine people struck a human note that was heard around the world—at least for a little while. Maybe you are too.

WHAT'S YOUR NAME?

So do we have the Catonsville Nine to thank for the existence of the Talking Heads among us? We can perhaps more conclusively conclude that one feat of attentiveness leads to another and that the world gets turned around one act of neighborliness at a time. Given the relative obscurity of the Berrigan witness in popular memory now and how far we are these days from their plainspoken proclamation of divine order over everyday human disorder, we might wonder as well how it is that we've come to expect so little of people who call themselves religious or Christian.

I'm never done seeing and understanding—that a move so seemingly radical as that of the Catonsville Nine is par for the course for communities that mean to seek right perception and just relationship in a hypermilitarized and hypermonetized world. When I was twenty-two years old and not many years past my Kroger parking lot epiphany, I had a degree of awareness concerning the existence of such communities, but there remained many a dot I had yet to see connected.

It was the summer of 1992, and having ferried and hitchhiked over from a YMCA outdoor center where I lived and worked in Northern Ireland, I sat in an enormous tent at the Greenbelt Arts Festival at Castle Ashby, where I listened to the priest-professor Henri Nouwen teach and pray and expound upon his vision of the life of the spirit lived in community. I reveled in his description of spiritual discipline, of Jesus's need for solitude, and his own stories of life in service to the members of the L'Arche community. But I was tripped up when, toward the end, a story of his time among the impoverished of Peru rolled into an indictment of the US government's role in paramilitary violence in Guatemala, El Salvador, and Nicaragua. I listened but didn't hear how the one had to do with the other, and my own sense of reality at the time was, I'll admit, unduly influenced by the hours I'd clocked in as an avid listener of the radio personality Rush Limbaugh.

I'm not sure what I had in mind, but I somehow felt the need—defensively minded young person that I was—to let him know that humanity's definition of justice might not always coincide with what I considered the true, pristine, real, capital "J" Justice of God—and that we mustn't presume. So I intercepted his exit, introduced myself, and mumbled my way through whatever it was I wanted to say as my enthusiasm quickly outran my verbal coherence.

"And what's your name again?" he asked with a smile and a steadfast refusal to remove his eyes from mine.

Flustered: "Um. David."

"Hello, David," he intoned in an alarmingly unhurried fashion. Nouwen then proceeded to ask me numerous questions about where I was from, how I'd found myself there, and all this with a generous commentary (leading to further questions) on all my responses. He'd stopped dead in his tracks and didn't seem at all inclined to be on his way until I'd had enough. Before I knew it, I felt somehow simultaneously bigger, calmed, relieved of a burden, and very much lifted to the height of a peer. I didn't feel knocked down by his words—that was, of course, what was really going on—any longer. Before I knew it, I was ready to let him go and did.

After he'd taken a few steps to be on his way, he turned around to say, "Oh. And what you said about justice—you're right."

I'm told that dignity isn't something you can give somebody. It's only something you can be kind or sensible enough to recognize because people have it already, in and about themselves, whether we choose to realize it or not. It's in us even when they we don't know it. And maybe we feel it most solidly in ourselves when someone's decided to act or speak in deep recognition of its presence. Nouwen made me feel my own dignity, and it was as if I was being inaugurated into the way of the gift and invited, once again, into a community of sanity marked by what the apostle Paul refers to as "humility of mind."

I'm told that dignity isn't something you can give somebody. It's only something you can be kind or sensible enough to recognize.

Such humility comes most naturally to us when we're possessed by a sense of righteous abundance and the better ordering of life it demands. If we think of it as an order to which we're invited to pay heed in all we say, do, and conceive, it's also a righteous abundance in which we find and lose ourselves all at once. It demands consistent acknowledgment of the seriousness and affection and interest with which the Divine, we are told, regards every human being who ever lived. It could lead a person to burn a few deadly pieces of paper or respond unanxiously to an anxious interrogator or seek reconciliation with someone who's murdered someone you love. Each day is an opportunity to bring a depth charge of righteousness to any interaction. If not now, when?

Not to single Nouwen out unhelpfully, because such gestures of love and interest have happened to me numerous times before and continue to happen since. But it seems clear to me that what passed between us—or what Nouwen graciously passed over to me—was a sense of holiness that I recognized in that moment and in the aftermoments. Holiness blooms and blossoms when we hear and heed, in our hurry and our weakness, in our depression and disinterestedness, the chother, loving others as we hope to be loved. By way of such holiness, a community of sanity is formed. Maybe it's as nearby as the nearest person who wishes someone would ask them a question.

9

STRANGE NEGOTIATIONS

We flipped a coin, okay? You and me. You and me! Coin flip is sacred.
—Jesse Pinkman to Walter White in *Breaking Bad*

"I don't think there's any problem with the church these days except all these *non*-churches," observed Eugene Peterson. No problem save the plain old fact of too few people committed to trying to think and live sanely and therefore righteously together with others, come what may. Can we still find a living witness among the living?

I think so. I see them everywhere, actually, and I place the person, the image, the direct action, the novel, the joke, the poem, the film, or the lyric in my attention collection sometimes called *church* whenever I find one. Earthseed is, from what I can discern, on offer practically everywhere, though it's only rarely successfully marketed. Maybe it can't be marketed. Regardless, I mean to amplify and partner with it wherever it appears in our interfaith future. This is Beloved Community, the ever-ancient, ever-new gathering of souls hell-bent on finding, reciting, handing down, and living up to what we might yet find to be of help in the life's work of thinking and living sanely or *insanely*, depending upon who's passing judgment.

The poet Fanny Howe is especially eloquent concerning the countercultural realism to which those who seek true religion are called: "You know that we all, no matter what we do, answer to the time we were born in. We *are* the time we inhabit. . . . This is the interesting part of being Catholic: The heresy that comes along with it. Indistinguishable from the rites is the rage, the arguing, the rebelling, the mind on alert. I like to be on alert. And I like to be in an atmosphere where people examine one more completely insane vision of the universe."[1]

A mind on alert won't settle for the deadly divides that destroy neighbor, neighborhood, and planet, and a mind on alert won't accept that the way things are is the way things have to be. The mind on alert is committed to overcoming every death-dealing division with the living out of prophetic consciousness in all matters. The fact of the reigning dysfunction wherever we turn is simply a call for renewed examination and a determined leaning in as we dream up better ways of conceiving our relationship to others. May we never be incurious when it counts. Maybe it always counts.

A mind on alert won't accept that the way things are is the way things have to be.

REALISTS OF A LARGER REALITY

The insightful essayist and chronicler of the Occupy movement, Nathan Schneider, describes the situation thus: "The circumstances of our world exceed the politics we're used to imagining for it."[2] Against the despair of the status quo, there remain so many vantage points for imagining the world more truly—that would be true religion—and for overturning the violent divisions with which we find ourselves unwittingly playing along.

What alternatives to everyday despair remain unseen and untapped?

What would it look like to not be forever on the run from aware-ness of complications?

Ursula Le Guin once named the good work to be done with rare wit on the occasion of receiving the Medal for Distinguished Contribution to American Letters. In the face of certain perceived inevitabilities, we get to try to be people who counter—in word and deed—the reigning hypnosis: "We live in capitalism, its power seems inescapable—but then, so did the divine right of kings." Take *that*, status quo. There's more: "Any human power can be resisted and changed by human beings." If we listen hard enough, we can hear the voices of people—they really are everywhere, though they're mostly not famous—who "can see alternatives to how we live now and can see through our fear-stricken society and its obsessive technologies to other ways of being, and even imagine some real grounds for hope. . . . [Those] who can remember freedom—poets, visionaries—realists of a larger reality."[3]

Oh, the realists of the larger reality! I want to be in that number! To be among those—on a trajectory *with* those—who proceed sanely in word and deed. There remain before us so many avenues to social creativity, to problematizing the sad old, same old reigning nomencla-tures with socially disruptive newness. Whenever we undertake this newness, whether in public or in secret, we manage, in Daniel Berrig-an's phrase, to seed something into history.[4]

The alternative is crushingly familiar. Sunday morning sings of love for God and weeping over the wonders of God's grace while destroying land and poisoning water. Our elected leaders add to the escalating lawlessness they once promised to rectify, carefully saying whatever they think they have to say and voting however they think they have to vote to continue to hold on to their supposed power and influence. We lay waste to neighbors near and far in the name of that oft-demonic misnomer, homeland security. "The greater a hypocrisy," essayist and artist Jaron Lanier decrees, "the more invisible it typically becomes."[5] But it seems to me that if we hope to resist, counter, and name these liturgies of murderous abstraction, we have to render visible—and be alive to—the social fact of religion. Doing so might be one of the nearest means we have for facing the facts. Because every fact is a function of relationship.

POETS ARE THE MOST SPECIFIC PEOPLE ON EARTH

In this work, Daniel Berrigan might be our most eloquent diagnostician of inherited dysfunction, those religious forms that enslave all the more deviously for going unscrutinized. Here, he seems to have in mind all the trappings of officialdom and expertise, whether in courthouses, board meetings, or situation rooms, and their subtle—but not so subtle—bindings. His sense of the loss of prophetic consciousness in these environments, of the way access requires that it be left at the door, is devastating:

> It is necessary above all to be concrete when we speak of these things. [People, even ostensibly good people] are commonly disposed to submit to the slavery of the actual; they literally cannot imagine themselves in any life situation other than the one in which they live. They inherit a style, a culture, a religion—and they prolong such forms—because they are there; useful, comfortable, logical, venerable. Their minds wear the costumes of their ancestors, a clothing that was once befitting, literally, but is now simply a folklore or a fakeout. So they call folklore a religion and a fakeout in adult life. And, alas, who shall disenchant them? But let it at least be said, as the Lord implies from His Roman courtroom, such lives as these must not make large claims to the truth.[6]

"What *is* truth?" Pontius Pilate asks Jesus in what appears to be a tone of mercenary cynicism, as if the very question is distasteful and impolitic and beneath the interest of those who matter. Who has *time* to be true anymore anyway? Why not play it safe and stick to the handed-down commands of the teleprompter? The always-alternative poetic demand a prophet like Berrigan makes of us is, for starters, to begin to find our mythological presumptions presumptuous by being awake to them. For Berrigan, this connecting of dots in the face of prevailing mythologies whose caretakers busy themselves in (and derive their status from) making sure such connections *aren't* made is the name of the human game in the worlds we're in.

Of Berrigan, Kurt Vonnegut once made the following claim: "For me Father Berrigan is Jesus as a poet. If this be heresy, make the most of it."[7] Let's do. The vocation Vonnegut spies in Brother Daniel is the one Berrigan sees in Jesus as that figure of the divine who is also, if it helps to conceive him this way, the most realistic human being who ever lived: "Jesus, by a method that was breathtakingly realistic and right, sought to break the universal dominion of Death over [women and] men."[8] The poetic-prophetic imagination that follows the lead of Jesus is, in this sense, a demythologizing force ever at work upon the prevailing, death-dealing mythologies that otherwise have their way on and in our lives to our seemingly endless detriment.

When we think of it this way, the culture we call poetry is human seriousness itself. It's the work of making all things new, bodying forth newness of life and living and social possibility. With perhaps such visions in mind, the poet Anthony Towne, who, with William Stringfellow, harbored Daniel Berrigan following the Catonsville action and up until his arrest, remarked, "It is my considered opinion that any society that locks up priests is sick, and any society that imprisons poets is doomed."[9] Against the prevailing delusions of our days, the poets, those realists of a larger reality, remind us of what, in the most life-giving sense, "normal living" requires. "If there is any love in it," normal living "is one long gorgeous and, no doubt, subversive conspiracy."[10] Larger-reality realists are our poet-practitioners who would instruct us all in being better caretakers of words, of what we do with words (consider, for a moment, all the wonderful and horrible things we do with words). In this sense, theirs is the work of social mindfulness: "Poets . . . are the most specific people on earth."[11]

KNOW THE SIZE OF YOUR VEHICLE

To think of realism in *this* way is to begin to live in the midst of all manner of difficult questions, but I would argue that this has always been the very joy set before us. The call to own our own perceived necessity—to describe it, to change our ways of thinking and living—is one with the call to love our neighbors as if they are ourselves, *because they are.* Ancient and wise authority assures us this is the case. And yet this same deep joy is a deep threat—or perceived as one—by interests that prefer to keep accounts of people, events, and doings liturgically unrelated and boundaried up. According to the prevailing delusions, to see all human activity as religious is to see the world illegally.[12] There are countless reasons to keep the world divided, to not *say* what we *see* and to settle for being silent prophets. But what if the reigning divisions are unwieldy *because* they're idolatrous, because they never actually serve human interest? In these matters, there is neither separation nor the possibility of critical detachment. Our inescapable network of mutuality—our common existence—is a living fact that can't be reasonably denied.

But in the feverish and defensive commitment to compartmentalization, deny it we often do. By drawing a line between our supposed convictions and our actual practices, we hold and exercise power without taking responsibility for it. But what we believe *is* what we do.

Our policies and our liturgies are one and the same. In the case of the United States, for instance, our neuroses reach across the world with tragic consequences. As the journalist Mark Danner observed of the American public's responsibility in light of the disclosures of the Senate Torture Report, our fear and ignorance are translated into someone else's pain.[13] My perverse imagination is someone else's social disaster. And when it comes to the complications—the reverberations—of my getting, spending, voting, and consuming, my existence is revealed to be a walking catastrophe of conflict avoidance of which I'm only occasionally conscious.

I think, too, of Reality Winner, a military veteran sentenced to four years in prison for an act of conscience undertaken on behalf of the American people. Charged under the Espionage Act, her decision to leak classified material concerning Russian interference in the presidential election of 2016 assisted a Senate investigation undertaken to ensure safer elections in 2018 and 2020. Betrayed by the US government (my government), her one wild and precious life was (and remains) somehow lost in the constellation of competing interests that vie for control of the meaning of America. As of this writing, Alexandria Ocasio-Cortez and Ilhan Omar are the only elected officials to publicly acknowledge her existence. The risk aversion of pundits, pastors, politicians, and anyone who could amplify and shed light on her story equals her crushed spirit. Even now, though no longer incarcerated, she's denied the right to tell her story on her own terms, a brave, thoughtful woman indefinitely consigned to dwell outside the sphere of what most Americans are willing to know about themselves and the government of "we, the people." Leveling with ourselves means looking hard at the strange negotiations we're up to amid the trauma we consent to and fund as we try to get by. In this sense, "I'm not political" is the new "I'm not responsible for anything happening around me."

That phrase "strange negotiations" comes from singer-songwriter David Bazan, who's blessed us with an album and a song by that name. A conscientious person in sentence and song, his good humor is compellingly intertwined with a determination to look hard at societal failures that are communal failures and that are also, of course, personal failures. It's as if he's never met a survival strategy or a coping mechanism he can't figure out how to lyricize.

A moment I witnessed when I was with Bazan in a van as he negotiated the busy streets of Nashville as he wanted to leave town in time to reach his next venue; he also wanted to give his vanful of violinists—the Passenger String Quartet—the chance to wash their clothes in a laundromat. With OxiClean detergent balls at the ready, he had just enough time to drop them off to see to their laundry before heading for another joint.

As we headed to exit, enter an oversized sport-utility vehicle trying to parallel park in slow, grating, and very nonexpert fashion. We waited for the space to clear. And without forgetting that there was a real, living person in the big and inconvenient truck, Bazan allowed himself some words in a quietly exhaled plea: "Know the size of your vehicle, man."

With this expression, whether spoken unto ourselves or others, is invitation to take stock and to level with ourselves concerning the scope of what we're up to. I file it next—maybe it's a counterweight—to the notorious saying "Mistakes were made," that eerie disavowal of the fact of my own doings and nondoings. We abdicate responsibility for the space we take up when we speak of decisions or actions as phenomena that occur apart from us. When we don't yield space, we can't function communally even as we momentarily pause and get swiftly back to business. To treat it as such is to deprive it of its life-giving, world-repairing power. Like grace, it gets to inform the whole of a life, every minute particular, if we're to know joy and the root of joy or be delivered from suffering and the root of suffering.

Perhaps there's a joy available to us in realizing we can't successfully separate ourselves from our chother, however it is we've sought to alleviate our anxieties. We don't finally get away with anything. Our existence simply will not be zoned off into separate sections. Maybe, at our core, we don't desire separation to begin with. Maybe we just thought we couldn't handle a vision of wholeness. Maybe all the excess complexity we mistook for chaos is actually good news.

More than a little bit in sync with the magnanimous, sacramental wit we spy in an artist like James Joyce, Daniel Berrigan and his ilk invite us to live in search of "the larger yes," the wider human affirmation that is often elusive but also often scandalously present in any given circumstance. We are invited, in all things, to "undertake an ethic of resurrection, and live according to the slight edge of life over death." What's resurrection? Exemplary Catholic that he is, Berrigan defines resurrection as "the hope that hopes on."[14]

WHAT DO WE VALUE?

When it comes to such an ethic, this larger yes, this seizing of that slight edge of life over death, the Berrigan witness, exemplary as it is, remains just the tip of the iceberg, or *a tip* among *many* icebergs. But the Berrigan standard often serves as the standard by which I judge my own Earthseed vision, one that fits the facts as I understand them, that makes my attention collection a collection worth sharing. The Berrigans reside among various voices I depend on to keep me from abstracting myself out of the life of the world. The name Berrigan sets me to thinking, sets me to wondering how I might be more thorough in the way I'm living my life, the manner in which I'm conceiving others. And more than any figure I can think of, he reminds me—and it's often a bit of a haunting—that I'm never not broadcasting my sense of perceived necessity.

A haunting, because there's many a strange negotiation in trying to be true, many a denial I'm apt to indulge in order to avoid the shame spiral that beckons when I note the distance between my big talk and my actual doings, my beliefs about myself and my general inaction. This is my witness, which is always answering the prickly, high-drama question of what it is I really value. What's more interesting and entertaining and laughable than that? What's more humiliating?

One of the deep thrills of the *Breaking Bad* television series is the way it lays this question bare in the lives of high-school science teacher Walter White and his former student Jesse Pinkman. In their partnership of methamphetamine production, everything begins, persists, twists, and ends as the means to some supposed, seemingly inarguably good end. All manner of horror is justified by having been done (it *had* to be done) for the "right" reasons. Absolute security in theory, we find, leads to everyday nihilism in practice. The joys of honest speech become intensely unavailable. And it's all . . . so . . . familiar. They hedge. They deny. They blame. But decisions *have* to be made; certain roles *have* to be played. Who'll *take care* of the situation? Who'll do the deed? In their division of labor, there's a new dilemma— sometimes many overlapping dilemmas—in every episode. Bond, from one harried moment to the next, is king. And as it is in our own lives, except even more so, for Walter and Jesse it's always a question of what they're willing to credit as binding. Propelled by perceived necessity, they will be bound to certain murderous acts. In one such instance, an agreed-upon coin toss leaves the task to Walt. Walt balks. Jesse recites the improvised creed, "We flipped a coin, okay? You and me. You and me!" And in a kind of desperate growl, "Coin flip is sacred."

It can take the edge off to see and hear yet one more sacred designation described so plainly and tragicomically, but we're kidding ourselves if we detach ourselves entirely from the strange negotiations of Jesse and Walt. We're all in it.

And for many of us, it's as if we're never not monetizing, never not forcibly forgetting our interdependence for fear it'll slow us down, never not worshipping in one way or another (coin flip is sacred!). Not everyone takes the Macbeth-like path of Walter White, whose desire for complete autonomy so narrows his sphere of the sacrosanct that there's hardly anything in it save his own will to power. But most of us eschew the minute particulars in the name of security and control, forgetting—again and again—that the little things *are* the big things. So much of our energy is devoted to the externalizing of responsibility. We reach out, as the saying goes, but

And for many of us, it's as if we're never not monetizing. in our haste, our sadness, and our fear, we often lose the ability to be present to one another. High drama everywhere. The little distancings, we find, add up over time. But the realizations and confessions and blessed breakdowns do too.

As it turns out, we're awash in complex reminders that, if we have ears to hear and eyes to see, reveal again that the abstractions of success, progress, power, and stability are not unambivalent indices. Upon examination, we will often find that the doings, policies, and investments that occur beneath them are, in fact, social evils, cult activities we come to find we can no longer approve lest we conspire in the degradation and diminishment of self and neighbor. There are multiple signs everywhere—some chronicled in these pages—that expose and critique these unexamined liturgies.

And within us there is that which draws us to anything that invites us to acknowledge the sham, anything that facilitates the realization that so many of our perceived have-tos, the faulty blueprints we've been given, are a carefully calibrated mirage that doesn't dignify or ennoble but instead sabotages our own sense of ourselves.

What's a front and what's real?
How might we let a little air in?

EVERYONE'S INVITED

As the essayist Hugh Kenner observes of the forms we honor with the names like *art*, *poetry*, *gospel*, or *apocalypse*, there is always that which "lifts the saying out of the zone of things said."[15] There is always that which puts beauty back in play, making us delight in the possibility of knowing it and calling us back to awareness of ourselves. These are the labors of the ancestors we choose, and they are ours to receive and pass on as the gifts of poetic thinking. This is what the poet Aimé Césaire describes as "that process which through word, image, myth, love, and humor establishes me at the living heart of myself and of the world."[16] We have deep and urgent need of such gifts if we're to be people of the long haul.

"The long haul" is a phrase I associate with Myles Horton of Savannah, Tennessee, teacher and cofounder of the Highlander Folk School. Among the realists of the larger reality I know of, he is one strong link between various figures, artisans of hopefulness in our time, whom we're woefully prone to place in separate eras, concerns, and issue-driven camps. The labels, as ever, don't work. They only pervert. Horton studied, learned, and strategized, for instance, with Rosa Parks and Dietrich Bonhoeffer, Pete Seeger and Septima Clark, to name a few. In our tendency to elevate individuals as heroes over movements, to the exclusion of the long haul—that slow, communal work of discernment upon which lived righteousness depends—we trade a sense of how we might make ourselves available to history in the here and now for fleeting praise and stunted admiration, words of "due respect" on which we never get around to following through. By only approaching history by way of caricature and "big players," we cut ourselves off from available insight as to how to be available to history now, and the literacy of wonder is lost on us.

Horton, who offered training in nonviolent direct action to Rosa Parks and Martin Luther King Jr. and John Lewis, believed education is a matter of acquainting people—individuals—with a deeper sense of their own moral power, their own genius, and their revolutionary intuition. He believed we have to credit one another *with* and lift one another *toward* a deeper social acumen and a deeper hungering and thirsting for righteousness than we're accustomed to sensing—than we've been taught to sense—within ourselves:

> I don't think you help people by keeping them enslaved to something that is less than they are capable of doing and believing. I was told one time during an educational conference that I was cruel because I made people who were very happy and contented, unhappy, and that it was wrong to upset people and stretch their imaginations and minds, and to challenge them to the place where they got themselves into trouble, became maladjusted and so on. My position was that I believed in changing society by first changing individuals so that they could then struggle to bring about social changes. There's a lot of pain in it, and a lot of violence, and conflict, and that is just part of the price you pay. I realized that was part of growth—and growth is painful. A plant comes through the hard ground and it breaks the seed apart. And then it dies to live again. I think that people aren't fully free until they're in a struggle for justice. *And that means for everyone.* It's a struggle of such importance that they are willing, if necessary, to die for it. I think that's what you have to do before you're really free. Then you've got something to live for. You don't want to die, because you've got so

much you want to do. The struggle is so important that it gives meaning to life.[17]

So much of what we know and celebrate within the *still-being-realized* geopolitical revolution, the social genius, internationally embodied, that calls itself *Beloved Community*, is evident in this passage. Horton maintained that there is that within every human being which longs for justice and that we aren't quite humanly or humanely literate till that longing becomes embodied in some way, till we enjoin ourselves—our bodies—to the enactment of right order, to the flourishing of others, which is ultimately our *own* flourishing—giving us a vision of the social pipeline. And a way of dwelling most meaningfully within it. Consider the long haul. Everyone's invited.

Everybody I know wants to be true. And despite the fear and the awkwardness, the fronting and the faking, and all the ways we do it badly, I suspect everyone deep down longs to at least pursue the possibility of being genuine. It's so rightly and righteously attractive. Everyone wants to have and dwell within meaning. *Sharing* meaning, though, and *giving* meaning are a slightly different dance from simply expressing your one self. It's funny to put it this way, but you were already doing that. Or as the poet Mary Karr puts it, "Poetry doesn't need self expression. The self has been expressed. You're standing in it."[18] You're soaking in it. We see and hear you. You can't bring your values—your faith or your supposed non-faith—suddenly into play. That program is already in progress. It was always already there, being voiced. Sometimes louder and sometimes clearer than you intended. Our witness, our perceived necessity, is underway. And, good news, you are not alone.

We can *give* voice anytime at all by listening to someone else, by paying them heed and perhaps trying to do justice to their voice by remembering, rehearsing what we've heard of theirs, with our own. And both paradoxically and maybe a little hilariously, we can't hear our own voice till we've entertained the fact of someone else. Voice doesn't happen in isolation. It can only occur in relationship, the space of the c*other*, the realm of communion. To be heard at all—to *mean* at all—requires communion.

Perhaps the community you have in view is dysfunctional, broken, embarrassing. Perhaps you have a proposal for it? A word of criticism? Come forth with your critique, but know you can't fix what you won't join. There's no healing a community of which you in no way see yourself a part. Maybe criticism and hospitality joined at the hip contain what's needed for a conversation to occur. There are so many ways to weave a common life, to hold together that which is in danger of being *dis*membered. To *re*member, in this sense, is to no longer stand alone and to aid others in no longer doing so. A critique can be a gift, but it need never be confused for a call to abandon the human circle. Are you bewildered? Others have been here before. And at the heart of bewilderment, there can be a seed of compassion.

> **Come forth with your critique, but know you can't fix what you won't join. There's no healing a community of which you in no way see yourself a part.**

"To what do I appeal when I want to convince myself that I am somebody?" the activist-mystic Howard Thurman once asked his congregation.[19] In what associations do we hope to derive our significance? Both questions speak to the question of communion, those reserves upon which we attempt to mean well together with others. We have so much, so many ancestors, so many artifacts, to come to our rescue when we sit still long enough to attend to this question.

If I could end—or begin to end—as I began, I'll note again that I'm regularly delivered from certain madness by certain loves. In the preceding pages, I've shared more than one. They include very unfamous people, family members, biblical prophets, rebel priests, science-fiction writers, playwrights, poets, and all manner of pop-culture artisans. By their collected lights, I try to love and write the vision, making it as plain as I can, believing that there remains a vision that doesn't lie for any and every time. And with love comes—or can come—what I take to be appropriate anxieties, worries over whether or not I dwell rightly and reverently within a continuum alongside those I love. Would Emily Dickinson find me a little sympathetic and funny? Would James Baldwin think me a tiny bit incisive? Would my life make sense to Walt Whitman and the prophet Isaiah? Would Shakespeare spy in me a kindred spirit? This, too, is a longing for the coherence without which I feel diminished and out of sync. I want to be—to have been—in line with a holy ordering. Maybe you do too.

Senses of the holy differ, but the longing for some form of order is universal. My favorite thinker in this regard is the poet Gregory Orr, who maintains the following: "Each of us needs to believe that patterns and structures exist and *can be made to exist*. To be human is to have a deep craving for order."[20] We crave—sometimes safely and sometimes dangerously—order. We expend entire lives in this hope. It's what we do.

I DON'T WANT COMMUNION

As I've mentioned, I've spent thousands of hours of my own life undertaking this ordering attempt in the buildings popularly referred to as churches. For much of my adult life, I've pulled my children along too. As a child, I used to stare at a white wall a few feet away from the preacher and attempt to redeem the time by whiling away the minutes trying to reimagine every last detail of the last movie I'd seen. This, it seemed to me, was an acceptable expenditure of imagination so long as I was there, trying to feel it, trying to be present to the communion that is the trying-to-be-faithful people whose life is *church* and which is from time to time housed in the church *building*.

When they were much younger, my children used to pass notes and draw on the bulletins with me, often suddenly required bathroom breaks, and rolled their eyes at me as I whisper-hissed at them to pay attention. In one such instance, I even placed my fingers on my son Sam's lips to get him to move his mouth to the words of a hymn we were singing. My brother leaned forward from behind us to say, "Tell your dad he needs to behave in church." I considered retorting that I'm never *not* trying to behave in church . . . or *as* church, but I kept it to myself.

Anyway, one Sunday, both sons having ducked out to supposedly use the bathroom, Sam appeared with a Dr Pepper he'd procured with change he had, unbeknownst to me, in his jacket pocket. I told him to finish it outside as quickly as he could and to then get his body back in there. The sermon was almost over. After the sermon concluded and Communion was underway, Peter—that bright articulator of the chother principle, whose middle name is, what else, Berrigan—made his way down the pew with a plaintive look. "Could I have fifty cents?" he ask-whispered.

"No," I mouthed. He'd seen Sam in the company of a soft drink and thought it only fair that he be accorded one as well. "We'll talk about it later."

"Please," he whispered.

"Save it," I said. "We're about to have Communion."

"I don't want Communion," he decreed in a wide-eyed whisper.

He immediately understood he'd crossed a certain line as sacred to me as any coin flip. No sense in being a silent prophet to my own child. "You and I need to have a conversation." I told him that if he didn't *want* Communion, I'd like for him to wait outside.

This is not a flattering story for me. Am I still the anxious pilgrim in the Kroger parking lot, wolfing down crackers and grape juice the better to somehow please—and stave off the everlasting wrath of—the Lord? What's the big deal?

There is that which remains a big deal, and despite my sincerity, this kind of behavior now strikes me as right at the edge (and even passed the line) of spiritual abuse. We had a longish conversation about being the people of God, and the meaning of Jesus's witness in life and in his acceptance of death, that he likely won't remember. But I do desperately hope he'll see the way of the gift—the gifts of God for the people of God and the gift *of* God that is the sweet social fact of other people, the Beloved Community (with or without crackers and grape juice). But I want him to perceive and receive the gift with all that he is. I want him to know and experience *himself* as gift.

I want my kids to know—destined to live in an often horrifically incurious age—I want them to be part of that peculiarly curious remnant upon whom little or nothing is lost, who love their chother as themselves, and who are purposefully lost in admiration for the beauty of the earth that affords them a living. I want them to *know joy*. I'll learn it from them as much as—probably more than—they'll learn it from me, but my hope is that they'll grow in their love for "the felt fact," as Susan Howe's puts it,[21] in all that they're up to and that it will guide their devotion in all the forms it takes.

Our devotion, after all, *takes form*. We're standing in it, walking through it, breathing it, holding it. What shall we do with it? Is it worthy? What form shall my devotion take today to be among the most specific people the world has ever seen, to imagine ourselves and others poetically and gratefully? And it isn't, in the popular and narrow sense, a *spiritual* vision of the world that's expected to be detached from the actual world. It's a vision that reflects the divine, that is present to and for the world just as water is present to the sea. It is to be carried over into everything. *Eucharist* means "thanksgiving." And maybe that is why I "forced" the conversation with my son, why I felt so desperate in that parking lot—because there is no deep access to life without gratitude. No right perception without the sense of connection and interdependence that necessitates gratitude. For me, that specific thanksgiving is one essential vision of how to hopefully inhabit the world. I, for one, depend on it.

LOVE IS INTELLIGENCE

Look around for a screen, a billboard, or a conversation overheard, and you may well hear the call to pay no attention to the man behind the curtain, the call to live in denial of relationship to the room, house, neighborhood, city, country, or world within which you live and move and have your being. But to live in such denial is to live in diminishment. It is to cut yourself off from your own life.

In the hope of resisting this widespread diminishing move, I propose a break with the denial strategy when it comes to religion (religion as thine but never mine), this unfortunate way of distinguishing oneself from others. Life is too short to pretend we're not religious. Life's too short to not be grounded in the hope that we would come to habitually view relationship—interrelation—as a fact and not an issue. The ancient intelligence available to us in the stories of sacred traditions—we might call them *myths* so long as doing so removes our sense of their investigative heft—presumes interrelation at every turn, but one reason we're lately so estranged from this intelligence is our knee-jerk denial of our religiosity, our own fellow humanness.

If we think of relation as the starting point of our politics, our policies, and the visions for how we mean to organize our lives and our resources, a gust of justice often follows. It is with this insight in mind that the German theologian-activist Dorothee Söelle reminds us that "the relationship between human beings is not to be understood merely as a possibility that is realized now and then."[22] It's rather a fact—the fact—to be lived into at all times. We get to operate out of the blessed realization that "the ego is not the final horizon of the self."[23] It isn't a matter of making such connections; it's the essential task of learning to see, in all things, the fact of connection. The fact, lest we forget, doesn't require our recognition.

Separation, we've noted, is the sham, an unlovely and unpoetic way of viewing and proceeding with our lives. Recognizing this brings us back to that place of finding others beautiful and interesting. When such moments don't work *as* work or tasks or anything borne of a sense of obligation, we meet the intersection of 4th and Walnut—a gasp of recognition, of empathy, and the difficult joy—which will often have to involve laughter—of realizing how much of what we thought we knew for sure and had squared away was exceedingly wrong. Wrong because we had yet to begin to see with the eyes of love.

There is no seeing, no understanding, without it, the poet Robin Blaser argues: "I don't think intelligence exists without love. Love is intelligence. What kind of intelligence would you have without love?"[24] It's love that makes it possible for us to look deep into the eyes of others and see ourselves, our chother, the deep awareness of relationship that puts the mind in full flower and gives rise to the compassion without which there is no hope.

This book has been—I hope it's been—the start of a whisper campaign. We get to unlearn—we *have to* unlearn—the habitual defensiveness that only ascribes religiousness to others. And along this trajectory, I call myself religious in an effort to be more exactly honest with myself concerning what I'm up to. I'm never not confessing my beliefs, my faith in one way or another. And, if I may be permitted a return to the plural, understanding ourselves to be just as religious as anyone and everyone else might afford us time, space, and vision with which to see ourselves more clearly and honestly, the better to grasp or begin to grasp—it's a life's work, after all—the deepest implications of what we're doing to ourselves and others.

This kind of self-understanding can clear a path toward the joys of conversion, finding ourselves born again toward that literacy of wonder we lose when we're primarily guided by fear and defensiveness and the lazy drive to disassociation—a literacy we begin to achieve anew when affinity, affection, and a sense of mutuality guide us in our regard for other people.

The joy of a changed mind, that new birth many of us are secretly hoping for most of the time, is extremely near—and always an invitation. It might be one conversation, one human face, away.

AFTERWORD

Watching my own words get published in book form is a joy. More joyous still is receiving the opportunity to reconsider, revise, and even repent of some of the positions I staked out not so many years ago. As I've reread my earlier manuscript, I've detected a bullying, high-handed tone—a certain pushiness—that doesn't sit well with me. I've also come to see how the rhetorical posture I assumed in regard to the ways people define religion can serve to enable spiritual abuse, a phenomenon I've been too slow to see within and on the peripheries of the groupings we call faith communities, as well as the ideology of Christian supremacy, which has come to run roughshod over the rights of people who aren't and must not become Christian, in my ostensibly free country in new and unexpected ways over the last five years.

The above paragraph contains two, two-word phrases that had yet to be formed on my lips until very recently:

Spiritual abuse.
Christian supremacy.

I have a saying (a bit of a mantra actually) that's at the heart of my recent resolve to speak aloud of both: nobody's an authority in someone else's experience.

Spiritual abuse is a form of violence, whether in speech or behavior, in which I try to deny someone the right to assess their own thoughts, feelings, or experiences without me or, more broadly, apart from the community or tradition I imagine I'm adhering or being true to. I don't have to be conscious of it to be guilty of it. It's subtly undertaken and subtly detected. To see it requires slowing the tape and discerning what I'm too prone to speed or rush past in my own words, attitudes, and actions. I can't see myself as a spiritually abusive person until I begin to detect my own quickening pulse, my own sense of hurry, haste, and defensiveness when confronted with incoming data that doesn't flatter me or favor the optics of the position I've taken, whether publicly or privately. It is, of course, grounded in a kind of fear.

A tragic and dramatic example can be discerned in the recordings we have of Jim Jones directing his followers within the Peoples Temple Agricultural Project to poison themselves and their families in November 1978. He accuses parents questioning his deadly directive of being unreasonable and needlessly upsetting their own children. He registers and responds to their words even as he also speaks over them. His ability to do both and to switch it up within a space of seconds is an audible demonstration of his rhetorical skill. For many of his hearers, he proves catastrophically capable of verbally vanquishing their own instincts for survival. "Quickly, quickly, quickly, quickly, quickly" he intones, urging them to bring their cups to their own lips and the lips of people they've loved without any further thought of betraying the effort they'd undertaken together.

How do we characterize this horror? How does one even begin to try to process or bear adequate witness to what occurred? Moments like these call for a steady commitment to accurate thinking. It will be important to recall that the world in which an exchange like this occurred is our world. There were perceived necessities in play. Religion names a horrible thing. It matters how we name a horrible thing. When I characterize the Peoples Temple tragedy (which came to be referred to as the "Jonestown Massacre") as a form of religion, I want to simultaneously characterize it as a form of politics lest assigning it with one label, but not the other, obscure the subject I have in mind. As I've argued, good analysis shows relationship. Bad analysis obscures it. If we're to learn, we have to go granular.

I bring up the Peoples Temple because echoes of the tragedy are referenced in one of the most effective examinations of spiritual abuse I've ever beheld: Mike Flanagan's television series, *Midnight Mass*. Fantasy is a form of scrutiny, and *Midnight Mass*, despite its dependence on vampire lore and demonology, offers a vision of how spiritual abuse occurs. Crockett Island is made up of admirable people, most of whom are members of a Catholic parish that tends to the needs of their community, including a Muslim sheriff and his son, as they each try to draw a living out of a threadbare economy wrecked by an oil spill.

There is nothing caricatured or cartoonish about their adherence to scripture and Roman Catholic liturgy or even the spirited conversation that ensues when the administration of the island's public school tries to proselytize the sheriff's son. Nevertheless, most of the characters, most of whom we've come to love and admire, subtly succumb to great evil. And as is perhaps always the case, the promise of security, control, and the overcoming of death is at the heart of the wicked bargain. There are ways to try to make right what went wrong, but there are no moral shortcuts to righteousness. As a work of grief, reckoning, and realism, *Midnight Mass* is on the level of Krzysztof Kieślowski's *Dekalog*.

There are dark sayings that arise in my consideration of the film that came to me as a revelation. They also speak to the themes of this book: We become what we agree to. We become what we consent to. We become what we play along with.

If I can quickly apply them to my own life, I'd like to confess to a defensiveness concerning the word *religion* that I now wish to renounce. I don't much like people with my background (in this case, white evangelical) being cast in an ominous light. But *ominous* is the word for what my culture has produced. About my people, I have been optimistic to the point of denial. And I don't want my wishful thinking to contribute to someone else's suffering one second longer. There are scholars, activists, and prophets who've helped me overcome my blind spots in this regard. I'd like to name and commend them to you here: Larycia Hawkins, Jazz Robertson, Justin Jones, Bree Newsome Bass, Chrissy Stroop, Anthea Butler, Reality Winner, Lisa Sharon Harper, and Kristin Kobes Du Mez.

Nobody's an expert in someone else's experience. I return to this assertion because it's something I believe **Nobody's an expert** I hadn't quite made my own as I wrote the **in someone else's** earlier version of this book. Within me was a fight concerning the word *religion*. In one **experience.** sense, it's still there. Exploring what forms of culture might become more visible to us if we choose to define religion as "perceived necessity" is still, to my mind, a worthy project, crucial even, insofar as defining religion this way makes space for increased moral scrutiny and transparency concerning, say, defense budgets, the prison-industrial complex, or taxpayer-funded terrorizing of asylum seekers. Similarly, when governors and state legislatures try to ban "divisive concepts" or critical race theory or the enunciation of the word *gay* in public education, they, too, are driven by perceived necessity. Talk of "traditional values," "biblical worldview," and generalized faith masks the raw fact of what many bad faith actors are up to. To get into it, to persistently ask the question "Faith in what, exactly?" of otherwise morally unaccountable people hiding behind the word *religion*, is essential. Generalization is tyranny's oxygen supply. Specificity cuts it off.

At the same time, the rhetorical move whereby a person insinuates that everybody's pushing a religion or an ideology of some sort at all times is a base one. Pundits, professional politicians, and political appointees deploy it to justify or excuse corruption. Terror successfully marketed or presented in court as religion is still terror. And compulsion in religion, which the Quran forbids, carried out under the presumption that religious indoctrination is unavoidable is still compulsion. I don't want to contribute to that sleight of hand for one second longer. I have an example.

"The dogma lives loudly within you," Senator Dianne Feinstein once observed of not-yet-then Supreme Court Justice Amy Coney Barrett in a Senate hearing. This moment was read by her supporters as a dig at Justice Barrett's Roman Catholic faith, and she was lionized as she eventually overcame opposition as a Trump appointee. But the scrutinizing of her public speech (on the part of journalists and Senate staff) to better discern ideological commitments was a matter of due diligence for anyone desirous of a genuinely pluralist republic, anyone opposed to compulsion in the matter of religion. In 2006, Justice Barrett had told graduates of Notre Dame Law School that their "legal career is but a means to an end." What end? "The building of the kingdom of God."[1]

One hears of bearing witness to the kingdom of God, seeking it, and, for instance, hungering and thirsting after righteousness, but if a person auditioning for the right to exercise legal power over others has decreed that their legal career is merely a means to building a kingdom not everyone credits as real or legitimate, a request for elaboration on that decree isn't an attack on their faith or anyone's religious liberty. This brings us to a worrying position I'd like to analyze.

"All schools in making choices about curriculum and the formation of children have to come from some belief system. And in public schools, the school boards, the districts are making that choice . . . the choice of classes to be taught and the kind of values that they want to inculcate in the students." This is Justice Barrett working her way toward a question for Christopher Taub, Maine chief deputy attorney general, in *Carson v. Makin.* I believe I hear a rhetorical sleight of hand in her words.

All schools, in making choices about content and curriculum in public education, *do not* have to come from "some belief system." "Belief system" is a catastrophically unhelpful pair of words for characterizing the myriad traditions of knowledge and inquiry that inform behavior and shape our sense of what we owe each other as citizens.

Religion names a thing. How we name a thing matters. We, the people of the United States, have a constitutional right to *not fund* any form of religious indoctrination or what Justice Barrett refers to as "building the kingdom of God." In fact, we have a responsibility (presuming we mean to uphold the Constitution) to not compel each other to fund religious indoctrination. And yes, after taxes, we're each perfectly free to fund as much religious indoctrination as we like.

Nobody's perceived necessity is uniform. To replace the word *religion* with *belief system* in these matters serves abusive ends. Our Supreme Court has a responsibility to rule against any effort to compel taxpayers to fund religious indoctrination. It is not the case that everybody's doing it or that all education is some form of indoctrination. If Justice Barrett was placed before a white supremacist sexual predator president as the right choice because of the language game she'd publicly committed to in her commencement speech, we have a right to know.

I have often been slow to see the violence implicit in that particular language game. My hope is that this book creates a space in which that violence is more, not less, visible. More, not less, talk about what we mean we speak when we speak of religion is essential to issues of national security, especially in view of the violence we've seen over the last five years in the form of white supremacist gerrymandering, the harassment and killing of Asian Americans, and one political party's attempt to overthrow the government on behalf of their outgoing president leader. It is too often the case that the perpetrators, pundits, and politicians involved in this violence have been baptized and catechized in our churches. It's high time to highlight and reckon with these connections, to look hard, humbly, and repentantly at the incoming data. It must not be denied.

I can easily *avoid* the language of spiritual abuse by speaking in terms of my own experience, admitting, at every turn, its limits, and declining to try to rhetorically universalize my feelings, my thoughts, my confession, and my position. I succumb to spiritual abuse when I center my own take, double down, and try to dictate for others how they ought to feel or where they're at. Religion names a thing. It matters how we name a thing. But I am not an authority in anyone else's experience. What a needless psychic pickle I'm in when I imagine otherwise.

Christian supremacy as an actual, sometimes taxpayer-funded form of terror in the world has been even harder for me to see, because I don't like to think of supremacy (or nationalism) as something that could ever be "Christian." Well, I'm done with that language game. It's no help at all when politicians protected by church organizations are targeting trans kids, disenfranchising nonwhite voters, and defunding public education while tweeting Bible verses. Christian supremacy is sneaky. We live in clarifying times.

Since the earlier edition came out, I've become more comfortable with looking at these phenomena squarely and saying what I see. I've been defensive over the Christian tradition when I've believed it was being misrepresented or needlessly maligned. That posture has been hurtful, I now understand, for those whose experience of the tradition differs from mine. I'm done playing that way. I'm exceedingly grateful for the opportunity to correct the written record and change my position. Repentance is the final human seriousness. And I have brought that seriousness to this edition.

In our one human barnyard, cultures of spiritual abuse are never fenced off from the workplace, the boardroom, or the world of unaccountable lobbyists and unaccountable lawmakers. I say this to recognize how abusive behavior and unprocessed trauma eventually take the form of corrupt policy. I hope my theory of religion serves to address this by focusing on the moral power available to each of us as we examine our interior lives as well as the life of collectives. The poet W. S. Merwin has a sobering but hopeful word for us here: "I don't think we can get rid of violence. Anger is in all of us. And greed is in all of us. We can't get rid of it in ourselves. We can't get rid of it in the society. But we can oppose the organization of it. The use of it as a tool, and as a threat."[2]

Religion is organized violence. But religion is also organized opposition to organized violence. There is so much good work to be imagined and undertaken in reconceiving our own sense of perceived necessity and the dubious claims of perceived necessity having their way in our world.

Hannah Arendt, who coined the word *totalitarianism* to name the total assault on every form of moral power in individuals and institutions, gives us a description of the mental and physical task of attempted constancy, matching the word to the deed and the deed to the word. Listen: *"Power is actualized only when word and deed have not parted company, where words are not empty and deeds are not brutal, where words are not used to veil intentions but to disclose realities, and deeds are not used to violate and destroy but to establish relations and create new realities."*[3]

It matters how we name a thing.

It matters how we name a thing. So much comes down to the language we consent to when we enter the commerce of conversation, what we behold, hear, and nod along with. I've been so gratified to hear tell of how this book has served as a kind of clearing for so many for whom religion has been a kind of nightmare from which they wish to awaken. May new realities, new forms of kinship, appear before of us in the heady days ahead.

On that note, I'd like to leave you with a word on method from the poet Denise Levertov. A little like Octavia Butler, she has a lovely way of speaking of divinity as a form of creative intuition without succumbing to the soft fascism of Christian supremacy. Because I believe the poet and the prophet are near allied—and sometimes practically synonymous—this passage fits the spirit I hope to urge, convey, and pass on to you, dear reader (please pardon the first-person masculine). Receive the oracle:

> The poet—when he is writing—is a priest; the poem is a temple; epiphanies and communion take place within it. The communion is triple; between the maker and the needer within the poet; between the makers and the needers outside him—those who need but can't make their own poems (or who do make their own but need this one too); and between the human and the divine in both poet and reader. By divine I mean something beyond both the making and the needing elements, vast, irreducible, a spirit summoned by the exercise of needing and making. When the poet converses with this god he has summoned into manifestation, he reveals to others the possibility of their own dialogue with the god in themselves. Writing the poem is the poet's means of summoning the divine.[4]

Hear here. Can you hear the oracle? See? You can do it too. Amplify the oracle always. Insert soul here.

ACKNOWLEDGMENTS

"Write what will stop your breath if you don't write," Grace Paley once advised. And I've found it takes a fellowship of curious people (at least one or two) to become and stay motivated in the direction of really doing it. So many sweet people have been consistently kind and inquisitive in helping me to lift up, articulate, and generally stick with what's often felt like nothing more than an odd little quibble over an unfashionable and off-putting word. To family and friends and faculty colleagues polite enough to sit still and listen as I tried to explain what I'm on about, I thank you. To students at the Tennessee Prison for Women, Riverbend Maximum Security Institution, and Belmont, Tennessee State, Lipscomb, and Vanderbilt Universities, I thank you for letting me know when I wasn't making any helpful sense and inviting me to try again and again. And for very specific help with the manuscript, I thank Carlene Bauer (whose exceedingly helpful questions gave me a title), J. T. Daly, David Zimmerman, Amy Caldwell, Cory Bishop, Dorothy Day Dark, and my friends in the Virginia Seminar in Lived Theology: Valerie Cooper, Shannon Gayk, Amy Laura Hall, Susan Holman, Russell Jeung, John Kiess, Jenny McBride, Charles Marsh, Vanessa Ochs, Peter Slade, and Shea Tuttle. I also want to communicate my gratitude to Todd Greene, who keeps me believing I have good words to offer, and Lil Copan, the best editor I know about, for helping me not disgrace myself in print and urging me to make the time to write my mind the way I want it to read.

NOTES

Introduction: Religion Happens

1   Karl Marx, "A Contribution to the Critique of Hegel's Philosophy of Right: Introduction," in *Marx: Early Political Writings*, trans. Joseph J. O'Malley (Cambridge: Cambridge University Press, 1994), 57.

2   David Byrne, *Bicycle Diaries* (New York: Viking Penguin, 2009), 2.

3   Elaine Scarry, *On Beauty and Being Just* (Princeton, NJ: Princeton University Press, 1999), 7.

4   Padraig O Tuama, "What Does It Mean to Pay Spiritual and Moral Attention to Conflicts in Our Lives?" https://www.americamagazine.org/faith/2019/09/20/what-does-it-mean-pay-spiritual-and-moral-attention-conflicts-our-lives.

5   I owe the phrase "oppositional energy" to my friend and mentor Dane Anthony of Nashville. As you might imagine, religion is a sometimes catastrophically difficult topic for many people who live in Tennessee.

6   Iris Murdoch, "The Sublime and the Good," in *Existentialists and Mystics: Writings on Philosophy and Literature*, ed. Peter Conradi (New York: Penguin, 1997), 215. With thanks to Sallie McFague for the tip.

Chapter 1: Crackers and Grape Juice

1   Neil Gaiman, *American Gods* (New York: HarperCollins, 2011), 450.

2   Teresa K. Weaver, "Maya Angelou's Final Chapter," Palm Beach Post-Cox News Service, May 5, 2002, www.racematters.org/mayaangeloufinalchapter.htm.

3   Hannah Arendt, "The Crisis in Education," in *Between Past and Future*, ed. Jerome Kohn (New York: Penguin, 2006), 193.

4 Joe Sacco and Art Spiegelman, "Only Pictures?" *Nation*, February 20, 2006.

5 Octavia Butler, "Positive Obsession," in *Bloodchild and Other Stories* (New York: Seven Stories Press, 1995), 127–133.

6 Octavia Butler, *Parable of the Sower* (New York: Grand Central Publishing, 1993), 219.

7 Butler, *Parable of the Sower*, 78.

8 James Joyce, *Stephen Hero* (New York: New Directions, 1944), 26.

9 Butler, *Parable of the Sower*, 42.

10 Octavia Butler, "Persistence," *Locus Magazine*, June 2000.

11 Butler, *Parable of the Sower*, 261.

12 G. E. Bentley Jr., *Blake Records* (Oxford: Clarendon Press, 1969), 310.

Chapter 2: Attention Collection

1 Albert Camus, *The Fall*, trans. Justin O'Brien (New York: Vintage, 1991), 111.

2 Elaine Pagels, *Beyond Belief: The Secret Gospel of Thomas* (New York: Vintage, 2004), 53.

Chapter 3: Choose Your Ancestors Carefully

1 The skit was written by Adam McKay, who would go on to direct Ferrell in *Anchorman* and write and direct the gift to our species that is *Don't Look Up*. The more I think about it, the more I imagine "Wake Up and Smile" is essentially a rough draft of *Don't Look Up*.

2 Ralph Ellison, *Shadow and Act* (New York: Random House, 1964), 145. This insight was conveyed to me with enlivening clarity by my mentor Hortense Spillers.

3 Ellison, *Shadow and Act*, 31.

4 Kurt Vonnegut, introduction to *Mother Night* (New York: Random House, 1966).

5   I borrow this way of putting it from Sam Dark's elaboration on Shakespeare's counsel from Sonnet 35.

6   David Gates, "Dylan Revisited," *Newsweek*, October 5, 1997, www.newsweek.com/dylan-revisited-174056.

7   Mary Rose O'Reilly, *The Barn at the End of the World* (Minneapolis: Milkweed Editions, 2000), 151.

8   Marilynne Robinson, *Gilead* (New York: Picador, 2004), 114.

9   John Darnielle, *Wolf in White Van* (New York: Farrar, Straus and Giroux, 2014), 99.

10 Darnielle, *Wolf in White Van*, 200.

11 Darnielle, *Wolf in White Van*, 132.

12 Darnielle, *Wolf in White Van*, 36.

13 Darnielle, *Wolf in White Van*, 22–23.

14 Darnielle, *Wolf in White Van*, 195–97.

Chapter 4: I Learned It by Watching You

1   *Dangerous Visions: 33 Original Stories*, ed. Harlan Ellision (New York: Doubleday, 1967), 215.

2   "Rod Serling," *American Masters*, December 29, 2003, www.pbs.org/wnet/americanmasters/episodes/rod-serling/about-rod-serling/702/.

3   George Eliot, *Middlemarch* (New York: Penguin Classics, 1994), 838.

4   Eliot, *Middlemarch*, 181.

5   Eliot, *Middlemarch*, 183.

6   Ursula K. Le Guin, *The Wind's Twelve Quarters: Short Stories* (New York: Harper and Row, 1975), 285.

7   Ursula K. Le Guin, *Dispossessed* (New York: Avon, 1974), 84.

8   Le Guin, *Dispossessed*, 247.

9   Le Guin, *Dispossessed*, 47.

10 Philip K. Dick, *The Shifting Realities of Philip K. Dick: Selected Literary and Philosophical Writings*, ed. Lawrence Sutin (New York: Vintage, 1996), 261.

11 Philip K. Dick, *The Transmigration of Timothy Archer* (New York: Simon & Schuster, 1982), 55.

12 Philip K. Dick, *The Three Stigmata of Palmer Eldritch* (New York: Doubleday, 1965), 36–37.

13 Douglas Gorney, "William Gibson and the Future of the Future," *Atlantic*, September 14, 2010. https://www.theatlantic.com/entertainment/archive/2010/09/william-gibson-and-the-future-of-the-future/62863/.

14 William Gibson, *The Peripheral* (New York: Putnam, 204), 481–482.

15 Kurt Vonnegut, *Mother Night*, vii.

Chapter 5: Hurry Up and Matter!

1 Adrienne Rich, "*Introduction*," in *A Muriel Rukeyser Reader*, ed. Jan Heller Levi (New York: Norton, 1994), xiv.

2 William Wordsworth, *Preface to "Lyrical Ballads*," www.bartleby.com/39/36.html. I owe my alertness to this application of this passage to Denis Donoghue, *On Eloquence* (New Haven, CT: Yale University Press, 2008), 11–12.

3 Jacques Ellul, *The Technological Bluff*, trans. Geoffrey W. Bromiley (Grand Rapids: Eerdmans, 1990), 364.

4 Stephen King, *Cell* (New York: Simon & Schuster, 2006), 329.

5 James Gibbons, "Beyond Recognition," *Bookforum*, September/October/November 2006, www.bookforum.com/inprint/013_03/555.

6 Quoted in John Madera, "O For a Muse of Fire . . . An Interview with Lance Olsen," *Rain Taxi*, Online Edition: Summer 2010, www.raintaxi.com/o-for-a-muse-of-fire-an-interview-with-lance-olsen/.

7 William Stafford, interview by Jeff Gundy, *Artful Dodge*, College of Wooster, OH, https://artfuldodge.spaces.wooster.edu/interviews/william-stafford/.

8 William Gibson, *Distrust That Particular Flavor* (New York: Penguin, 2012), 44.

9 Patton Oswalt, "Wake Up, Geek Culture. Time to Die," *Wired*, December 27, 2010, www.wired.com/2010/12/ff_angrynerd_geekculture/all/.

10 I owe this articulation to Rob and Kirstin Vander Giessen-Reitsma, the founders of *culture is not optional. The community they cultivate and sustain by way of the Huss Project in Three Rivers, Michigan, is, to my mind, an alive and signaling witness to Beloved Community.

Chapter 6: Be the Religion You Want to See in the World

1 Kathy L. Gilbert, "Lawson: Black Lives Matter, a Religious Movement," *United Methodist News*, July 23, 2020, https://www.umnews.org/en/news/lawson-black-lives-matter-a-religious-movement?fbclid=IwAR3iTrHZBpl VlJSAFzTltNtxMyufhA2Qmcot9_uOybICjNEBqR1sqVhfjOk.

2 "'Nones' on the Rise," *Pew Research Center*, October 9, 2012, www.pewforum.org/2012/10/09/nones-on-the-rise/.

3 Stan Lee and Steve Ditko, "The Possessed!," *Strange Tales*, March, 1964, 118, collected in *Marvel Masterworks* 1, http://marvel.wikia.com/wiki/Strange_Tales_Vol_1_118.

4 Martin Luther King Jr., "Letter from a Birmingham Jail," April 16, 1963, audio letter, Stanford University, https://kinginstitute.stanford.edu/king-papers/documents/letter-birmingham-jail.

5 *Sourcebook of the World's Religions: An Interfaith Guide to Religion and Spirituality*, ed. Joel Beversluis (Novato: New World Library, 2000), 289.

6 Marilynne Robinson, *Gilead* (New York: Picador, 2004), 66.

7 Wendell E. Berry, "It All Turns on Affection," National Endowment for the Humanities 2012 Jefferson Lecture, www.neh.gov/about/awards/jefferson-lecture/wendell-e-berry-lecture.

8 Wendell Berry, "Two Economies," *World Wisdom Online Library*, www.worldwisdom.com/public/viewpdf/default.aspx?article-title=Two_Economies_by_Wendell_Berry.pdf.

9   James 1:27.

10   "Vincent Harding—Civility, History, and Hope," *On Being with Krista Tippett*, May 22, 2014, www.onbeing.org/program/civility-history-and-hope/79.

11   Desmond Tutu, *No Future Without Forgiveness* (New York: Doubleday, 1999), 31. The germ of this chapter, a welcome intersection of the insights of Wendell Berry and Desmond Tutu, came to me through an unpublished essay by Jacob Harris, an incarcerated philosopher and activist who resides in the Turney Center Industrial Complex.

12   Søren Kierkegaard, *Fear and Trembling*, trans. Walter Lowrie (Princeton, NJ: Princeton University Press, 1968), 21.

Chapter 7: The Chother

1   George Monbiot, "The Self-Attribution Fallacy," *Guardian*, November 7, 2011, www.monbiot.com/2011/11/07/the-self-attribution-fallacy/.

2   Thomas Merton, *Conjectures of a Guilty Bystander* (New York: Doubleday, 2009), 156.

3   Wendell Berry, "The Responsibility of the Poet," in *What Are People For?* (New York: North Point Press), 90.

4   Berry, "The Responsibility of the Poet," 90.

5   *Mishna Avot* 1:14.

6   This question arose in my failure to adequately paraphrase an insight articulated by Jaron Lanier in *Who Owns the Future?* (New York: Simon & Schuster, 2013), 31.

7   Daniel Berrigan, *Jeremiah: The World, the Wound of God* (Minneapolis: Fortress, 1999), 23.

8   Ralph Ellison, *Invisible Man* (New York: Vintage International, 1995), 581.

Chapter 8: Policy Is Liturgy Writ Large

1   Rebecca Solnit, "Call Climate Change What It Is: Violence," *Guardian*, April 7, 2014, www.theguardian.com/commentisfree/2014/apr/07/climate-change-violence-occupy-earth.

2   Sarah Kendzior, "The Telegenically Dead: Why Israel and Its Support-
    ers Fear Gaza's Dead," *Aljazeera*, August 14, 2014, www.aljazeera.com/
    indepth/opinion/2014/08/telegenically-dead-20148118231287o982.html.

3   Teju Cole, Twitter post, April 30, 2014, 7:18 a.m., https://twitter.com/tejucole.

4   Daniel Berrigan, quoted in Walter B. Kalaidjian, *Languages of Liberation:
    The Social Text in Contemporary American Poetry* (New York: Columbia
    University Press, 1989), 164.

5   Daniel Berrigan, *Wisdom: The Feminine Face of God* (London: Sheed &
    Ward, 2002), 61.

6   Claudia Luther, "Philip F. Berrigan, 79; Priest and Pacifist Who Helped
    Inspire Vietnam War Protests," *Los Angeles Times*, December 8, 2002,
    http://articles.latimes.com/2002/dec/08/local/me-berrigan8.

7   Daniel Berrigan, *To Dwell in Peace: An Autobiography* (San Francisco:
    Harper & Row, 1987), 201–2.

8   Berrigan, *To Dwell in Peace*, 201–2.

9   Berrigan, *To Dwell in Peace*, 219–20.

10 Berrigan, *To Dwell in Peace*, 221.

11 Daniel Berrigan, *Consequences: Truth and . . .* (New York: Macmillan, 1967), 78.

12 Daniel Berrigan, "Introduction," in *The Time's Discipline: The Beatitudes
    and Nuclear Resistance*, eds. Philip Berrigan and Elizabeth McAlister
    (Baltimore: Fortkamp, 1989), xx.

13 Daniel Kreps, "David Byrne Can't Vote but Hopes You Will," *Roll-
    ing Stone*, November 4, 2008, www.rollingstone.com/music/news/
    david-byrne-cant-vote-but-hopes-you-will-20081104.

Chapter 9: Strange Negotiations

1   Kim Jensen, "Fanny Howe," *BOMB*, Winter 2013, http://bombmagazine.
    org/article/6925/fanny-howe.

2   Nathan Schneider, *Thank You, Anarchy: Notes from the Occupy Apocalypse*
    (Berkeley: University of California Press, 2013), 74.

NOTES

3   Ursula K. Le Guin, "Speech in Acceptance of the National Book Foundation Medal," November 19, 2014, www.ursulakleguin.com/NationalBook FoundationAward-Speech.html. Copyright © 2014 Ursula K. Le Guin.

4   Daniel Berrigan, *Absurd Convictions, Modest Hopes: Conversations after Prison with Lee Lockwood* (New York: Random House, 1972), 107.

5   Jaron Lanier, *Who Owns the Future?* (New York: Simon & Schuster, 2013), 14.

6   Daniel Berrigan, *No Bars to Manhood* (Garden City, NY: Doubleday, 1970), 55.

7   Daniel Berrigan and Adrianna Amari, *Prayer for the Morning Headlines: On the Sanctity of Life and Death* (Baltimore: Apprentice House, 2007), cover.

8   Daniel Berrigan, "Preface," in *Suspect Tenderness*, eds. William Stringfellow and Anthony Towne (New York: Holt, Rinehart, and Winston, 1971), 7.

9   Stringfellow and Towne, "On Sheltering Criminal Priests," in *Suspect Tenderness*, 22.

10   Stringfellow and Towne, "On Sheltering Criminal Priests," 31.

11   Stringfellow and Towne, "On Sheltering Criminal Priests," 48.

12   Daniel Berrigan, *And the Risen Bread: Selected Poems*, ed. John Dear (New York: Fordham, 1998), 230.

13   "We translated our ignorance into their pain. That is the story the Senate report tells." Mark Danner and Hugh Eaken, "The CIA: The Devastating Indictment," *MarkDanner.com*, February 5, 2015, www.markdanner.com/ articles/the-cia-the-devastating-indictment.

14   Daniel Berrigan, "An Ethic of Resurrection," in *Testimony: The Word Made Flesh*, ed. John Dear (Maryknoll, NY: Orbis, 2004), 220–221.

15   Hugh Kenner, *A Homemade World: The American Modernist Writers* (New York: Knopf, 1975), 60.

16   Aimé Césaire, introduction to *Lyric and Dramatic Poetry, 1946–1982*, trans. Clayton Eshleman and Annette Smith (Charlottesville: University Press of Virginia, 1990), lv.

17   Myles Horton with Judith Kohl and Herbert Kohl, *The Long Haul: An Autobiography* (New York: Teacher's College Press, 1998), 184. I'd like to thank Michael Gagné, who shared this passage with me. Italics mine.

18 Mary Karr, Twitter post, November 22, 2013, 8:06 a.m., https://twitter. com/marykarrlit.

19 Howard Thurman, "Barren or Fruitful?," in *A Strange Freedom: The Best of Howard Thurman on Religious Experience and Public Life*, ed. Walter Earl Fluker and Catherine Tumbler (Boston: Beacon Press, 1999), 23.

20 Gregory Orr, *Poetry as Survival* (Athens: University of Georgia Press, 2002), 16. Italics mine.

21 Susan Howe, *Souls of the Labadie Tract* (New York: New Directions, 2007), 9.

22 Dorothee Soelle, *Mystery of Death*, trans. Nancy and Martin Lukens-Rumscheidt (Minneapolis: Fortress, 2007), 79.

23 Soelle, *Mystery of Death*, 111.

24 Douglas Todd, "Hippest Man on Earth," *Vancouver Sun*, September 6, 2008, www.canada.com/vancouversun/news/westcoastnews/story. html?id=7936ead0-aa9e-4c87-a3e0-4c2333e1c564&p=4 Robin Blaser.

Afterword

1 Associate Professor Amy Coney Barrett, Diploma Ceremony Address, https://scholarship.law.nd.edu/cgi/viewcontent.cgi?article=1013& context=commencement_programs.

2 Christian McEwen, "An Interview with W. S. Merwin," *The Writer's Chronicle*, February, 2015, 47. I owe my awareness of this quote to H. L. Hix.

3 Hannah Arendt, *The Human Condition* (New York: Anchor Books, 1959), 178–179.

4 Denise Levertov, *The Poet in the World* (New York: New Directions, 1973), 47.